PYTHON FOR DATA SCIENCE

2 BOOKS IN 1.
PHYTHON CRASH COURSE +
PHYTHON FOR DATA ANALYSIS

A PRACTICAL BEGINNER'S GUIDE
TO LEARN PYTHON PROGRAMMING,
INTRODUCING INTO DATA ANALYTICS,
MACHINE LEARNING, WEB DEVELOPMENT,
WITH HANDS-ON PROJECTS

ERICK THOMPSON

TABLE OF CONTENTS

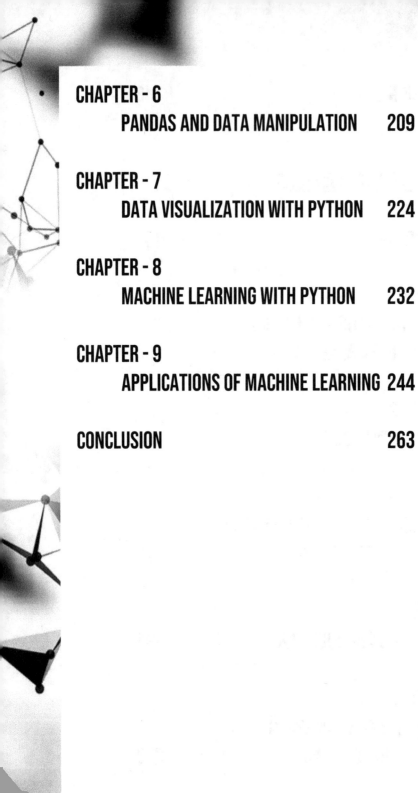

PHYTHON CRASH COURSE

A PRACTICAL BEGINNER'S GUIDE TO
LEARN PYTHON IN 7 DAYS OR LESS,
INTRODUCING YOU INTO THE WORLD
OF DATA SCIENCE, ARTIFICIAL
INTELLIGENCE AND MACHINE
LEARNING, WITH HANDS-ON
PROJECTS

ERICK THOMPSON

INTRODUCTION

Python is a significant level programming language, normally utilized for general purposes. It was initially developed by Guido van Rossum at the "Middle Wiskunde and Informatica (CWI), Netherlands," during the 1980s and presented by the "Python Software Foundation" in 1991. It was planned essentially to underscore comprehensibility of programming code, and its linguistic structure empowers developers to pass on thoughts utilizing less lines of code. Python programming language speeds up activity while taking into account higher productivity in making framework reconciliations. Designers are utilizing Python for "web advancement (server-side), programming improvement, arithmetic, framework scripting."

With the presentation of different upgrades, for example, "list appreciation" and a "trash assortment framework," which can gather reference cycles, the Python 2.0 was propelled in the last quarter of 2000. Thusly, in 2008,

Python 3.0 was discharged as a significant rendition overhaul within reverse similarity taking into consideration the Python 2.0 code to be executed on Python 3.0 without requiring any adjustments. Python is bolstered by a network of software engineers that ceaselessly create and keep up the "CPython," which is an open-source reference usage. The "Python Software Foundation" is a not revenue driven association that is liable for overseeing and coordinating assets for creating Python programming just as "CPython."

Here is a portion of the key highlights of Python that render it as the language of decision for coding beginners as well as advanced programming software engineers alike:

1. Readability: Python peruses a great deal like the English language, which adds to its simplicity of coherence.

2. Learnability: Python is a significant level programming language and considered simple to learn because of the capacity to code utilizing the English language like articulations, which infers it is easy to appreciate and, in this way, become familiar with the language.

3. Operating Systems: Python is effectively open and can be worked across various Operating frameworks including

Linux, Unix, Mac, Windows among others. This renders Python as an adaptable and cross-stage language.

4. Open Source: Python is an "open source", which implies that the engineer network can flawlessly make updates to the code, which are consistently accessible to anybody utilizing Python for their product programming needs.

5. Standardized Data Libraries: Python includes a major standard information library with an assortment of helpful codes and functionalities that can be utilized when composing Python code for information examination and advancement of AI models.

6. Free: Considering the wide appropriateness and use of Python, it is difficult to accept that it keeps on being openly accessible for simple download and use. This suggests anybody hoping to learn or utilize Python can just download and utilize it for their applications totally complimentary. Python is in reality an ideal case of a "FLOSS (Free/Libre Open Source Software)", which implies one could "uninhibitedly convey duplicates of this product, read its source code and alter it."

7. Supports overseeing special cases: An "exemption" can be characterized as "an occasion that can happen during program exemption and can disturb the typical progression of the program." Python is fit for supporting the treatment

of these "exemptions," inferring that you could compose less blunder inclined codes and test your code with an assortment of cases, which might prompt a "special case" later on.

8. Advanced Features: Python can likewise bolster "generators and rundown appreciations."

9. Storage administration: Python is likewise ready to help "programmed memory the executives," which infers that the capacity memory will be cleared and made accessible consequently. You are not required to clear and let lose the framework memory.

Applications:

1. Web planning – Some of the generally utilized web structures, for example, "Django" and "Flagon" have been created utilizing Python. These structures help the designer recorded as a hard copy server-side codes that empower the board of database, age of backend programming rationale, planning of URL, among others. AI – An assortment of AI models has been composed solely in Python. AI is a path for machines to compose rationale so as to learn and fix a particular issue all alone. For example, Python-based AI calculations utilized being developed of "item proposal frameworks" for eCommerce organizations, for example, Amazon, Netflix, YouTube and

some more. Different cases of Python-based AI models are the facial acknowledgment and the voice acknowledgment innovations accessible on our cell phones.

2. Data Analysis – Python can likewise be utilized in the advancement of information perception and information investigation instruments and procedures, for example, disperse plots and other graphical portrayals of information.

3. "Scripting" – It can be characterized as the way toward producing basic projects for mechanization of direct undertakings like those required to send robotized email reactions and instant messages. You could build up these sorts of programming utilizing the Python programming language.

4. Gaming Industry – A wide assortment of gaming programs have been created with the utilization of Python.

5. Python additionally bolsters the advancement of "implanted applications."

6. Desktop applications – You could utilize information libraries, for example, "Tinder" or "QT" to make work area applications dependent on Python.

CHAPTER - 1

THE WORLD OF DATA SCIENCE

TECHNOLOGIES

Data science

If you work with data, then Data Visualization is an important part of your daily routine. And if you happen to use Python programming language for your analysis, you must be overwhelmed by the sheer number of choices available in the form of data visualization libraries

How to Generate Data

Data visualization includes numerous equipment for generating information. The equipment used in the technology of visualized records in Python include the following:

Cluvio

Ever needed for a device that may permit the introduction of thrilling visualizations? Cluvio might be the device which you have been looking for. Cluvio is a corporation based totally in Germany that was founded in 2016. It offers thrilling and excellent features for its users and allows you to execute SQL queries from your database.

More than 100 groups accept as true with this tool of records visualization due to various reasons:

Amazing usability and design. Cluvio has an exquisite design for its customers this is of good excellent and an easy interface for the novice Python programmers to apprehend. The design has high requirements that allow the advent of interactive models. Supports the analysis of SQL-primarily based records. It analyzes any structured

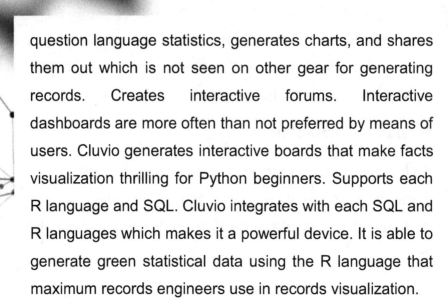

question language statistics, generates charts, and shares them out which is not seen on other gear for generating records. Creates interactive forums. Interactive dashboards are more often than not preferred by means of users. Cluvio generates interactive boards that make facts visualization thrilling for Python beginners. Supports each R language and SQL. Cluvio integrates with each SQL and R languages which makes it a powerful device. It is able to generate green statistical data using the R language that maximum records engineers use in records visualization.

This makes the tool greater famous than different tools.

Suitable for each small and huge organizations. Cluvio consists of various pricing alternatives that desire both the infant organizations and the major agencies. It has an unfastened pricing option plan, a starter plan, and also a seasoned plan for the big corporations. Each of the plans has different features for its users.

One of the downsides of Cluvio is that it does no longer help different file codecs which include the CSV and the Excel formats.

Google charts

You have all heard of Google, proper? Google offers sizable tools for its users across the world that help within the running and execution of facts. A Google chart is one of the equipment being presented that assists you in your management and in the presentation of information. Google charts constitute and generate your statistics inside the shape of pie charts and pictographs. This makes it simpler for customers to examine the records and make the evaluation. Google charts are unfastened gear that makes them popular compared to other equipment which can be provided at a rate.

Moreover, Google charts do no longer require any programming abilities so as to use them. It normally favors the amateur Python programmers who do no longer have adequate programming skills in view that they're just starting up their programming journey. They are capable of generating visualized information from statistical graphs and pie charts.

Google charts also offer the benefit of free virtualization hosting for its users at no cost. This enables the sharing of data across the website. Google charts also allow programmers to generate on their photographs from charts and different plots by the use of an API (Application Programming Interface) referred to as the Image Charts API. With this API, you're best required to set up a URL on the way to include your statistics on the facts and its formatting. You do no longer require any type of coding to be able to generate a photo from a Google chart.

Its main downside is that it has a poor guide for its clients, in contrast to other gear of data visualization. Also, there might also be possibilities of the loss of your images in situations in which the Google servers are down. Many of the beginner Python programmers suffer this on the grounds that they neglect to again up their images. The final drawback of a Google chart is that it denies its customers the capability to carry out a few modifications on their code since the code isn't quite exposed.

Infogram

This is a device used to generate information from advertising. It has excessive competencies for publishing compared to the equipment cited above. In fogram is much famous for its simplicity to apply because it contains a person-friendly interface for the newbie Python programmers to apprehend. It additionally offers terrific help for customers in contrast to its far visible on other gear together with the Google charts. In fogram is normally preferred with the aid of the managers and the software engineers involved in the information virtualization.

Infogrames focus on pix as a way to generate statistics. They offer its customers with templates that permit customization based on the statistical information and any sort of pix. It is obtainable at a rate of approximately $19 per person every month. This makes it incorrect for not the well-established firms. Its performance isn't quite functional compared to a different gear.

Visme

This is a device used for the design of shared stories in a manner of shows. Visme consists of three pricing plans which encompass the individual plan, the enterprise plan, and the education plan. Most people utilize this device due to its simple user interface that provides ease of use. Visme also provides extensive graphs and resources that assist within the advent of stable and attractive models. It additionally offers good high-quality customer support that allows in supporting the novice Python programmers.

The downside concerned for this tool include troubles with the text boxes and varying fine of the layout while files are exported. This makes it tough for beginners to use. Individuals who mostly opt for this tool are the advertising directors and also the persons involved in media productions.

Flare

This is an ActionScript library that allows customers to create any form of virtualization from the charts to something interactive. Flare permits you to make displays of the charts in an affordable manner. Users additionally have the capability of creating customizations at the

dashboards via using text bins on the way to point out the insights.

The downside of this tool is that the virtualization made while using this device is quite flawed for cellular packages. It is additionally hard to integrate this device with a few website programs. Mores, the flare device takes time to be up to date and it, therefore, produces outdated dashboards not forgetting the many bugs it contains.

How to Download Data?

Gone are the times when maximum of the amateur Python programmers experienced tough times while downloading their visualized records. It has been thankfully made less complicated nowadays to attract your records with the aid of imposing some modules. The modules being talked about right here are Pandas and Matplotlib.

Let us now get into details at the numerous modules to help you download your Python records.

Pandas

They are Python packages with several tools for analyzing records.

Pandas are used for the management and importation of datasets in Python using lots of codecs. They also are included with some of the strategies which can assist within the fact's analysis in Python.

Many individuals choose the use of pandas in facts visualization because of the following reasons:

They allow facts presentation in a manner that may be without problems analyzed. They do this via the usage of the Series statistics structure and also Data Frame records structure.

Pandas encompass a number of techniques suitable for the efficient filtering of data.

They additionally contain a fixed of utilities that guide the enter and output operations. Pandas can study the distinctive formats of facts such as CSV and additionally MS excel.

How can you put it in pandas?

Pandas do now not include the regular Python distributions. You need to put in them to your terminal to use them. This can be accomplished by the usage of the pip command that typically comes with the Python distribution. Run the pip command together with pandas on the terminal of your system.

In conditions where you have got anaconda already set up on your gadget, you could run the conda command

collectively with the pandas for your terminal to make the set up successful. You are advised to put in the trendy version of pandas for your gadget. You are now equipped to go.

Let us now dig deeper into the styles of data systems noted above that are used by pandas in Python.

Series

This form of information structure is similar to a one-dimensional array. A series of information systems gives garage to any sort of information, and its values can't be changed. The first detail of the information shape is normally assigned an index fee of 0 while the ultimate element is assigned an index of N-1. N represents the total amount of factors within the information structure.

To first establish the Pandas collection:

You want to import the pandas' bundle to your terminal.

Series is then created with the aid of the usage of an array after calling on the pd. Series () technique.

The contents of the Series will finally be displayed after walking at the print () command.

The output of the content material will include columns, whereby the primary column can be the indexes of the

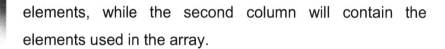

elements, while the second column will contain the elements used in the array.

A collection also can be generated by using the use of the numpy array then, later on, made some conversion to a Pandas series. This is how it may be accomplished.

#import on pandas on your terminal.

#import on numpy.

#import on the system command.

#call on the file object for the output to be displayed by the print () method.

#call on the numpy library to create an array of your elements #assign an array to the Pandas series.

#call on the print method to display the output.

The output will contain a primary column with the indexes of the factors, and the second column can be elements of your array.

Data Frame

This form of facts shape in pandas is in the shape of a desk that displays information within the phrases of rows and columns. It is a 2-dimensional array, in contrast to what is visible inside the Series records shape. The values

of the columns may be changed without affecting their identities.

Data Frame records systems can be generated from scratch, or you may determine to use on the numpy library and convert them later to the facts structure.

By constructing from scratch, you could follow the subsequent steps:

#import pandas in your terminal #create a Data Frame.

#assign Data Frame to a variable the use of pandas wherein you furthermore may assign the values of the rows and columns as part of your arguments. #name at the print method to show the output.

CHAPTER - 2

CUSTOMER TARGETING AND

SEGMENTATION

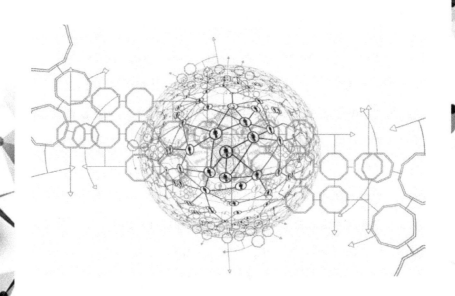

For the advertising organizations to have the option to arrive at their clients with an elevated level of personalization, they are required to target progressively granular sections. The man-made

brainpower innovation can draw on the current client information and train Machine learning calculations against "highest quality level" preparing sets to recognize normal properties and critical factors. The information sections could be as basic as area, sexual orientation, and age, or as perplexing as the purchaser's persona and past conduct. With AI, Dynamics Segmentation is attainable which represents the way that clients' practices are ever-changing, and individuals can take on various personas in various circumstances.

Deals and Marketing Forecast

One of the clearest computerized reasoning applications in promoting is in the advancement of deals and advertising gauging models. The high volume of quantifiable information, for example, clicks, buys, email reactions, and time spent on website pages fill in as preparing assets for the AI calculations. A portion of the main business knowledge and creation organizations in the market are Sisense, RapidMiner, and Birst. Advertising organizations are constantly overhauling their promoting endeavors, and with the assistance of AI and AI, they can anticipate the accomplishment of their showcasing activities or email crusades. Man-made consciousness innovation can examine past deals information, monetary patterns just as industrywide correlations with foresee short and long-haul deals execution and estimate deals results. The business conjectures model guide in the estimation of item request and to assist organizations with dealing with their creation to upgrade deals.

Automatic Advertisement Targeting

With the presentation of computerized reasoning innovation, offering on and focusing on program-based commercial has gotten essentially increasingly effective. Automatic publicizing can be characterized as "the mechanized procedure of purchasing and selling promotion stock to a trade which interfaces sponsors to distributers." To permit constant offering for stock across web-based social networking stations and cell phones just as TV, man-made reasoning innovation is utilized. This likewise returns to prescient examination and the capacity to display information that could beforehand just be resolved retroactively. Man-made consciousness can help the best time to serve a specific promotion, the likelihood of an advertisement transforming into deals, the responsiveness of the client, and the probability of commitment with the advertisement.

Automatic organizations can assemble and investigate visiting clients' information and practices to streamline ongoing efforts and to focus on the crowd all the more correctly. Automatic media purchasing incorporates the utilization of "interest side stages" (to encourage the way toward purchasing advertisement stock on the open market) and "information the executives' stages" (to give the promoting organization a capacity to arrive at their intended interest group). So as to enable the promoting rep to settle on educated choices with respect to their planned clients, the information the executive's stages are intended to gather and break down the enormous volume of site "treat information." For instance, web crawler showcasing (SEM) publicizing rehearsed by channels like Facebook, Twitter, and Google. To productively oversee tremendous stock of the site and application watchers, automatic promotions give a critical edge over contenders. Google and Facebook fill in as the best quality level for productive and powerful publicizing and are equipped to words giving an easy to understand stage that will permit non-specialized advertising organizations to begin, run and measure their drives and crusades on the web.

Visual Search and Image Recognition

A long way of the progressions in man-made brainpower-based picture acknowledgment and examination innovation has brought about uncanny visual pursuit functionalities. With the presentation of innovation like Google Lens and stages like Pinterest, individuals would now be able to discover results that are outwardly like each other utilizing the visual hunt usefulness. The visual inquiry works similarly as customary content put together quests that show results with respect to a comparable theme. Significant retailers and promoting organizations are progressively utilizing the visual pursuit to offer an improved and all the more captivating client experience. Visual pursuit can be utilized to improve promoting and give item suggestions dependent on the style of the item rather than the buyer's previous conduct or buys.

Significant ventures have been made by Target and Asks in the visual quest innovation advancement for their web-based business site. In 2017, Target reported an organization with intrigue that permits incorporation of Pinterest's visual pursuit application called "Pinterest focal point" into Target's portable application. Accordingly, customers can snap a photo of items that they might want to buy while they are all over town and find comparable things on Target's online business website. Essentially, the visual pursuit application propelled by Asks called "Asks' Style Match" permits customers to snap a photograph or transfer a picture on the Asks site or application and quest their item index for comparative things. These apparatuses draw in customers to retailers for things that they may run over in a magazine or while making the rounds by helping them to look for the perfect item regardless of whether they don't have the foggiest idea what the item is.

Picture acknowledgment has hugely helped showcasing organizations to increase an edge via web-based networking media by permitting them to discover an assortment of employments of their image logos and items in staying aware of the visual patterns. This wonder is additionally called "visual social tuning in" and permits organizations to distinguish and get where and how clients are collaborating with their image, logo, and item in any event, when the organization isn't alluded straightforwardly by its name.

Marketing and Advertising

An AI calculation created because of enormous information investigation can be effortlessly prepared with writings, stills, and video portions as information sources. It would then be able to extricate articles and ideas from these sources and suggest effective showcasing and publicizing arrangements. For instance, an apparatus called "Laban" was created by Alibaba that can make pennants at lightning speed in contrast with a human originator. In 2016, for the Chinese web-based shopping spectacle called "Singles Day," Laban produced a hundred and 17 million standard structures at a speed of 8000 pennant plans for every second.

The "twentieth Century Fox" teamed up with IBM to utilize their AI framework "Watson" for the making of the trailer of their blood and gore film "Morgan." To gain proficiency with the fitting "minutes" or clasps that ought to show up in a standard thriller trailer, Watson was prepared to group and examine input "minutes" from various media and other piece components from over a hundred thrillers. This preparation brought about the production of a six-minute film trailer by Watson in a minor 24 hours, which would have taken human expert weeks to create.

With the utilization of Machine learning, PC vision innovation, common language preparing, and prescient examination, the promoting procedure can be quickened exponentially through an AI showcasing stage. For instance, the man-made consciousness based promoting stage created by Albert Intelligence Marketing can produce self-ruling effort the board procedures, make custom arrangements and perform crowd focusing on. The organization revealed a 183% improvement in client exchange rate and over 600% higher discussion effectiveness credited to the utilization of their AI-based stage.

In March 2016, the computerized reasoning based innovative executive called "man-made intelligence CD ß" was propelled by McCann Erickson Japan as the primary

mechanical inventive chief at any point created. "Man-made intelligence CD ß" was given preparing on select components of different TV shows and the victors from the previous 10 years of All Japan Radio and Television CM celebration. With the utilization of information mining capacities, "simulated intelligence CD ß" can extricate thoughts and subjects satisfying each customer's individual crusade needs.

CHAPTER - 3

APPLICATION OF MACHINE LEARNING

UTILIZING SCIKIT-LEARN LIBRARY

To see how Scikit-Learn library is utilized in the improvement of machine calculation, let us utilize the "Sales_Win_Loss informational index from IBM's

Watson vault" containing information acquired from deals battle of a discount provider of car parts. We will fabricate a Machine model to anticipate which deals crusade will be a champ and which will bring about misfortune.

The informational index can be imported utilizing Pandas and investigated utilizing Pandas methods, for example, "head (), tail (), and types ()." The plotting procedures from "Seaborn" will be utilized to imagine the information. To process the information Scikit-Lean's "preprocessing. Label Encoder ()" will be utilized and "train_test_split ()" to separate the informational collection into preparing subset and testing subset.

To create expectations from our informational index, three unique calculations will be utilized, to be specific, "Straight Support Vector Classification and K-closest neighbors' classifier." To think about the exhibitions of these calculations Scikit-Learn library procedure "accuracy score" will be utilized. The presentation score of the models can be imagined utilizing Scikit-Learn and "Yellow brick" perception.

Importing the Data Set

To import the "Sales_Win_Loss informational index from IBM's Watson archive," initial step is bringing in the "Pandas" module utilizing "import pandas as pd."

At that point we influence a variable URL as "https://community.watsonanalytics.com/wp content/transfers/2015/04/WA_Fn-UseC_-Sales-Win-Loss.csv" to store the URL from which the informational index will be downloaded.

Presently, "reads () as sales data = predocs (URL)" procedure will be utilized to peruse the above "csv or comma-isolated qualities" record, which is provided by the Pandas module. The csv record will at that point be changed over into a Pandas information structure, with the outcome in factor as "sales data," where the system will be put away.

For new 'Pandas' clients, the "pd.read csv()" method in the code referenced above will produce a plain information structure called "information system", where a record for each line is contained in the main section, and the name/name for every segment in the principal line are the underlying segment names obtained from the informational collection. In the above code scrap, the "business information" variable outcomes in a table delineated in the image beneath.

In the chart over, the "row0, row1, row2" speaks to singular record list, and the "col0, col1, col2" speak to the names for singular segments or highlights of the informational index.

With this progression, you have effectively put away a duplicate of the informational collection and changed it into a "Pandas" system!

Presently, utilizing the "head () as Sales_data. head ()" procedure, the records from the information structure can be shown as appeared beneath to get a "vibe" of the data contained in the informational index.

Data Exploration

Since we have our own duplicate of the informational index, which has been changed into a "Pandas" information outline, we can rapidly investigate the information to comprehend what data can tell can be assembled from it and appropriately to design a strategy.

In any ML venture, information investigation will in general be an exceptionally basic stage. Indeed, even a quick informational collection investigation can offer us critical data that could be barely noticeable something else, and this data can propose noteworthy inquiries that we would then be able to endeavor to answer utilizing our venture.

Some outsider Python libraries will be utilized here to help us with the handling of the information so we can effectively utilize this information with the amazing calculations of Scikit-Learn. Indeed, "(head)" is viably fit for doing substantially more than showing information records and redo the "head ()" procedure to show just a chose records with orders like "sales data. head(n=2)". This order will specifically show the initial 2 records of the informational collection. At a snappy look clearly segments, for example, "Supplies Group" and "Locale" contain string information, while segments, for example, "Opportunity Result," "Opportunity Number" and so on are included whole number qualities. It can likewise be seen that there are one of a kind identifiers for each record in the' Opportunity Number' segment.

Correspondingly, to show select records from the base of the table, the "tail () as sales data. tail ()" can be utilized.

To see the various information types accessible in the informational collection, the Pandas strategy "dtypes () as sales data. dtypes" can be utilized. With this data, the information segments accessible in the information structure can be recorded with their individual information types. We can make sense of, for instance, that the segment "Supplies Subgroup" is an "object" information type and that the segment "Customer Size by Revenue" is a "whole number information type." So, we have a comprehension of segments that either contain number qualities or string information.

Data Visualization

Now, we are through with fundamental information investigation steps, so we won't endeavor to manufacture some engaging plots to depict the data outwardly and find other covered stories from our informational collection.

Of all the accessible Python libraries giving information representation highlights, "Seaborn" is outstanding amongst other accessible choices, so we will utilize the equivalent. Ensure that python plots module gave via "Seaborn" has been introduced on your framework and fit to be utilized. Presently follow the means underneath create wanted plot for the informational collection:

Stage 1 - Import the "Seaborn" module with order "import seaborn as sns".

Stage 2 - Import the "Matplotlib" module with order "import matplotlib. pyplot as plt".

Stage 3 - To set the "foundation shading" of the plot as white, use order "sns.set (style="whitegrid", color-codes=True)".

Stage 4 - To set the "plot size" for all plots, use order "sns.set(arc= {'figure. fig size':(11.7,8.27)})".

Stage 5 – To create a "count plot", use order "sns. count plot ('Route to Market', data=sales_data,hue = 'Opportunity Result')".

Stage 6 – To expel the top and base edges, use order "sns.despine(offset=10, trim=True)".

Stage 7 – To show the plot, , use order "plotplt.show()".

Fast recap - The "Seaborn" and "Matplotlib" modules were imported first. At that point the "set ()" method was utilized to characterize the unmistakable attributes for our plot, for example, plot style and shading. The foundation of the plot was characterized to be white utilizing the code piece "sns.set (style= "whitegrid," shading codes= True)." Then the plot size was characterize utilizing order "sns.set(rc={'figure.figsize':(11.7,8.27)})" that characterize the size of the plot as "11.7px and 8.27px".

Next the order "sns. countplot ('Route To Market', data= deals information, hue='Opportunity Result')" was utilized to create the plot. The "count plot()" method empowers production of a check plot, which can open various contentions to modify the tally plot as per our prerequisites. As a feature of the first "count plot ()" contention, the X-hub was characterized as the section "Course to Market" from the informational collection. The following contention concerns the wellspring of the informational index, which would be "sales data" information system we imported before. The third contention is the shade of the structured presentations that was characterized as "blue" for the section named "won" and "green" for the segment named "misfortune."

Data Pre-Processing

From the information investigation step, we set up that larger part of the sections in our informational collection are "string information," however "Scikit-Learn" can just process numerical information. Luckily, the Scikit-Learn library offers us numerous approaches to change over string information into numerical information, for instance, "Label Encoder()" procedure. To change straight out names from the informational index, for example, "won" and "misfortune" into numerical qualities, we will utilize the "Label Encoder()" method.

The principal picture contains one section named "shading" with three records to be specific, "Red," "Green" and "Blue." Using the "Label Encoder()" strategy, the record in the equivalent "shading" segment can be changed over to numerical qualities, as appeared in the subsequent picture.

We should start the genuine procedure of transformation now. Utilizing the "fit change()" strategy given by "Label Encoder()," the names in the downright segment like

"Course To Market" can be encoded and changed over to numerical names practically identical to those appeared in the outlines above. The capacity "fit change()" requires input marks recognized by the client and thusly Will result in encoded names.

To know how the encoding is cultivated, how about we experience a model rapidly. The code occasion beneath comprises string information as a rundown of urban communities, for example, ["paris," "paris," "tokyo," "amsterdam"] that will be encoded into something equivalent to "[2, 2, 1,3]".

Stage 1 - To import the necessary module, use order "from sklearn import preprocessing."

Stage 2 - To make the Label encoder object, use order "le = preprocessing.LabelEncoder()".

Stage 3 - To change over the unmitigated sections into numerical qualities, use order:

"encoded_value = le.fit_transform(["paris", "paris", "tokyo", "amsterdam"])"

"print(encoded_value) [1 1 2 0]"

What's more, there you have it! We simply changed over our string information names into numerical qualities. The initial step was bringing in the preprocessing module that offers the "Label Encoder()" strategy. Followed by

CHAPTER - 4

DATA SCIENTIST: THE SEXIEST JOB IN THE 21ST CENTURY

The funny thing is that this great value of the data contrasts with that precisely the data is the most abundant resource on the planet (it is estimated that 2.5 trillion bytes of new information is created per day). They don't seem easy to make things compatible. How is it

possible that something so abundant is so valuable? Even if it was pure supply and demand, accumulating data should be trivial. And it is, the complex thing is to process them.

Until relatively recently we simply couldn't do it. At the end of the 90s, the field of machine learning began to take on an autonomous entity, our ability to work with immense amounts of data was reduced and the social irruption of the internet did the rest. For a few years we have faced the first great 'democratization' of these techniques. And with that, the boom of data scientists: nobody wants to have an untapped gold mine.

In search of a data scientist

The problem is that, suddenly, there has been a great demand for a profile that until now practically did not exist. Remember that you need statistical knowledge that a programmer does not usually have and computer knowledge that a statistician does not usually even imagine.

Most of the time it has been solved with self-taught training that completes the basic skills that the training program should have but does not have. That is why, today, we can find a great diversity of professional profiles in the world of data science. According to Burtch Works , 32% of active data scientists come from the world of mathematics and statistics, 19% from computer engineering and 16% from other engineering.

How to train?

Degrees:

Today, there are some double degrees in computer engineering and mathematics (Autonomous University of Madrid, Granada, Polytechnic University of Madrid, Polytechnic University of Catalonia, Complutense, Murcia Autonomous University of Barcelona) or in computer science and statistics (University of Valladolid) that seem the best option if we consider this specialization.

Postgraduate

The postgraduate is a very diverse world. We can find postgraduate, masters or specialization courses in almost all universities and a truly excessive private offer. To give some examples we have postgraduate degrees at the UGR, the UAB , the UAM , the UPM or the Pompeu Fabra. However, in postgraduate courses it is more difficult to recommend a specific course.

We must not forget that most of the work of data scientists is in companies that seek to make their databases profitable, because what market orientation is highly recommended. In fact, many of the masters in 'big data' are offered by business schools such as OEI or Instituto Empresa.

MOOCS

One of the most interesting resources you can find are the moocs (you know, the massive open online courses). In fact recently, we saw that this self-training option could have a lot of future. Starting with the specialization program in Big Data of Coursera, we can find online courses from the best universities in the world. All this without mentioning the numerous tools to learn languages like Python or R.

What languages should be learned?

In reality, as any initiate knows, in programming the choice of one language or another is always complicated. In this election they intervene from technical or formative factors to simple personal preferences. What is clear is that there are some languages more popular than others.

Although common sense tells us that each language is better for certain things, in practice there is a certain rivalry . Personally, I use R but I usually recommend Python. Not only because it is prettier, but because it is multipurpose and that is always an advantage.

Other tools

A fireproof

- Excel: It is not a language and usually does not like those who work with professional data. Or so they say when asked why polls say otherwise: 59% percent of respondents routinely use excel. So, finally, the application of Office spreadsheets is still a lot of war.

The corporate brother and other languages and programs

- Some languages or environments enjoy some success driven by corporate inertia: it is the case of the classic Matlab but progressively it is losing weight and use up to only 6%.

- If we examine the surveys we can find many more languages that obey more particular needs of the practice of data scientists (or the programs they use): Scala (17%), Slack (10%), Perl (12%), C # (6%), Mahout (3%), Apache Hadoop (13%) or Java (23%).

- Also, although it is possible that we should talk about them separately, there are many specific programs (free or proprietary) that are used in data science with different uses. For example, we could talk about Tableau, RapidMiner or Weka.

The labor market: salaries and opportunities

Salaries, as in general in the world of software development, change a lot depending on the place, the functions and the employer. However, right now it is a well-paid expertise. On a general level and according to the annual KdNuggets survey, salaries / incomes average $ 141,000 for freelancers, 107,000 for employees, 90,000 for government workers or in the non-profit sector; 70,000 dollars for work in universities.

However, these average salaries must be taken with great caution. While the average salary in the United States is between $ 103,000 and $ 131,000, in Western Europe it is between $ 54,000 and $ 82,000. In Spain, we are in similar numbers because, despite our (increasingly smaller) deficit of product companies, we have large companies (especially banks) that have turned in this field.

What differentiates data science from the rest of the development world is perhaps the shortage of professionals. This phenomenon makes salaries relatively inflated and, as more dater profiles appear, they adjust. Therefore, it can be said that it is time to get on the wave of data science.

CHAPTER - 5

USING METHODS

String literals are usually surrounded by single quotation marks and double quotation marks. For example, the world expression 'string' is written in

the same way as "string." You can print it in the shell with the print() function, just like I did with the data types in Python shell. The first step is to assign a string to some variable of your choice. You can write down the name of the variable that you want to use, which can be followed by the equal sign and then the string. Please note that you can use either a single alphabet or a full name as the name of a variable. Use them wisely in a program so that when you read the code, you know the job of each variable.

```
>>> myString = "I am learning deep learning with python."

>>> print(myString)

I am learning deep learning with python.

>>> myString = "I am studying deep learning with python."

>>> print(myString)

I am studying deep learning with python.

>>> myString = """I am studying deep learning,

with Python,

and I am really enjoying it,

and writing programs with it."""

>>> print(myString)
```

```
I am studying deep learning,

with Python,

and I am really enjoying it,

and writing programs with it.

>>> myString = '''I am studying deep learning,

with Python,

and I am really enjoying it,

and writing programs with it.'''

>>> print(myString)

I am studying deep learning,

with Python,

and I am really enjoying it,

and writing programs with it.

>>>
```

Like many programming languages, Python strings are like byte arrays, which represent Unicode characters. There is no character data type in Python. However, a single character is a string that has a length of 1. You can use square brackets to access elements of the string.

```
>>> myString = """I am studying deep learning,

with Python,

and I am really enjoying it,

and writing programs with it."""
>>> print(myString[10])

i

>>> print(myString[1])

>>> print(myString[2])

a

>>> print(myString[0])

I

>>>
```

Do you love slicing? Slicing always has a satisfying effect on the human brain. Python strings offer you the freedom to return a wide range of characters with the help of using the slice syntax. The first step in this regard is to specify the starting index and the ending index. Separate the two by a colon to return a part of the string.

```
>>> myString = """I am studying deep learning,

with Python,
```

```
and I am really enjoying it,

and writing programs with it."""
>>> print(myString[20:35])

earning,

with P
>>> print(myString[10:35])

ing deep learning,

with P
>>> print(myString[0:50])

I am studying deep learning,

with Python,

and I am
>>>
```

Python allows you to slice a string by using negative indexing as well. Let's see how you can do that. The only difference is that you will use negative numbers in the string.

```
>>> myString = """I am studying deep learning,

with Python,
```

and I am really enjoying it,

and writing programs with it."""

```python
>>> print(myString[-50:-1])
 really enjoying it,

and writing programs with it
>>> print(myString[-60:-1])

,

and I am really enjoying it,

and writing programs with it
>>> print(myString[-70:-10])
ith Python,

and I am really enjoying it,

and writing program
>>>
```

You can calculate the total length of a string by using the following code.

```python
>>> myString = """I am studying deep learning,
with Python,

and I am really enjoying it,
```

```
and writing programs with it."""

>>> print(len(myString))

100

>>>
```

String Methods

The first method that will come under discussion is the strip() method that does the job of removing whitespaces from your string at the start or the end.

```
>>> myString = """  I am studying deep learning,

with Python,

and I am really enjoying it,

and writing programs with it.  """

>>> print(myString.strip())

I am studying deep learning,

with Python,

and I am really enjoying it,

and writing programs with it.

>>>
```

In the following example, I will try three different methods on the same string. One method is to convert the text into a lower case; the second is to convert it into the upper case, while the third is to convert the text into title case. All of them are simple and very handy when you are composing messages that you have to display for your users.

```
>>> myString = """I am studying deep learning,

with Python,

and I am really enjoying it,

and writing programs with it."""

>>> print(myString.lower())

i am studying deep learning,

with python,

and i am really enjoying it,

and writing programs with it.

>>> print(myString.upper())

I AM STUDYING DEEP LEARNING,

WITH PYTHON,

AND I AM REALLY ENJOYING IT,
```

AND WRITING PROGRAMS WITH IT.

```
>>> print (myString.title())
```

I Am Studying Deep Learning,

With Python,

And I Am Really Enjoying It,

And Writing Programs with It.

```
>>>
```

Let's talk about some more string methods to learn how it operates.

```
>>> myString = """I am studying deep learning,
```

with Python,

and I am really enjoying it,

```
and writing programs with it."""
>>> print(myString.replace("studying", "reading"))
```

I am reading deep learning,

with Python,

and I am really enjoying it,

and writing programs with it.

```
>>> print(myString.replace("really", " "))
```

```
I am studying deep learning,

with Python,

and I am   enjoying it,

and writing programs with it.
>>> print(myString.replace("really", ""))
I am studying deep learning,

with Python,

and I am  enjoying it,

and writing programs with it.
>>> print(myString.replace("studying",""))
I am  deep learning,

with Python,

and I am really enjoying it,

and writing programs with it.
>>>
```

In the above example, I attempted to replace a word with a new word. Then I moved on to eliminating a word by replacing it with no word. I tried it thrice to explain how you can manage extra whitespaces that are likely to happen if you don't fix them. The best method is to eliminate extra spaces from the code. There is a special method known as the split() method that can split the string into several substrings.

```
>>> myString = """I am studying deep learning,

with Python,

and I am really enjoying it,

and writing programs with it."""

>>> print(myString.split(","))

['I am studying deep learning,' '\nwith Python,' '\nand I am
really enjoying it,' '\nand writing programs with it.']

>>> myString = "I, am, studying, deep, learning."

>>> print(myString.split(","))

['I', ' am', ' studying', ' deep', ' learning.']

>>>
```

There is another interesting method using which you can check if a certain phrase or a character exists in a particular string or not. There are two keywords 'in' or 'not in' that you can use for this method.

```
>>> myString = "I am studying deep learning."

>>> a = "studying" not in myString
```

```
>>> print(a)

False

>>> a = "studying" in myString

>>> print(a)

True

>>>
```

If you can recall the data types that I have shared with you earlier on, you will realize that Python is communicating with you in the Boolean data type. You have got the answer in False and True to your query. This method is the way to extract more information about a Python string through a specific method.

If you have got two strings, you can combine them easily by using the Python string concatenation method. The primary operator that you can use here is the '+' operator. Let's see how to do that.

```
>>> myString = "I am studying deep learning."

>>> myString1 = "with Python."

>>> combstring = myString + myString1

>>> print(combstring)

I am studying deep learning. with Python.
```

```
>>> myString = "I am studying deep learning."

>>> myString1 = " with Python."

>>> combstring = myString + myString1

>>> print(combstring)

I am studying deep learning with Python.

>>>
```

The above code snippet has two similar code examples. The first one has a flaw. There is no whitespace in the first after the word learning. Two words have been wrongly combined. I fixed the issue by adding whitespace at the start of the second string. This formula will be helpful for you when you are combining two strings for writing a program. This method is the easiest; however, there is another method that you can use to add necessary space between two strings. Both play the same role, so it is up to you which one you like the most.

```
>>> myString = "I am studying deep learning."

>>> myString1 = "with Python."

>>> combString = myString + " " + myString1

>>> print(combString)

I am studying deep learning with Python.
```

You can format your string at will by the following method. Formatting a string means that you can combine two data types when you are writing a program for a user. If you try to concatenate them by using the same technique that we used for two strings, this is unlikely to work for you. Let's see what happens when you try to do that.

```
>>> myString = 23
>>> myString1 = "I am John and I am " + myString
Traceback (most recent call last):
  File "<pyshell#98>", line 1, in <module>
    myString1 = "I am John and I am " + myString
TypeError: can only concatenate str (not "int") to str
```

Don't worry. There is a special method for this purpose, the format() method. This method picks up the passed arguments, formats them, and then adds them to the string where you put in the placeholders {}. Let's see how to insert numbers.

```
>>> myString = 23
>>> myString1 = "I am John and I am {}"
```

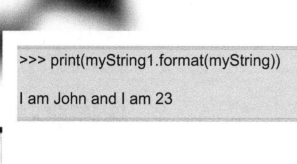

```
>>> print(myString1.format(myString))

I am John and I am 23
```

CHAPTER - 6

MACHINE LEARNING

This is going to be an essential part of our data analysis because it helps us to work with some of the algorithms and the models that we want to control in this process. With the help of machine learning and the use of the Python language that we talked about earlier, we are able to see our algorithms actually work and do some of the insights and predictions that we want to work with along the way.

To help us see why machine learning can be useful to our data analysis, we need to take a closer look at how machine learning is going to work in the first place.

What is Machine Learning?

The first thing that we need to take a look at here is the basics of machine learning. This is one of the approaches that we can use with data analytics that will help teach a computer how to learn and react on their own, without the interaction of the programmer. Many of the actions that we will train the system to do will be similar to actions that already come naturally to humans, such as learning from experience.

The algorithms that come with machine learning are going to be able to use computational methods in order to learn information right from the data, without having to rely on an equation that is predetermined as its model. The algorithms are going to adaptively improve some of their own performance as the number of samples that we will use for learning will increase.

With the rise in big data that is available for all industries to use, we will find that machine learning is going to become

one of the big techniques that are used to solve a ton of problems in many areas, including the following:

1. Computational finance: This is going to include algorithmic trading, credit scoring, and fraud detection.

2. Computer vision and other parts of image processing. This can be used in some different parts like object detection, motion detection, and face recognition.

3. Computational biology. This is going to be used for a lot of different parts, including DNA sequencing, drug discovery, and tumor detection.

4. Energy production. This can be used to help with a few different actions like load forecasting and to help predict what the prices will be.

5. Manufacturing, aerospace, and automotive options. This is going to be a great technique to work with when it comes to helping with many parts, including predictive maintenance.

6. Natural language processing: This is going to be the way that we can use machine learning to help with applications of voice recognition.

Machine learning and the algorithms that they control are going to work by finding some natural patterns in the data that you can use, including using it in a manner that will help us to make some better predictions and decisions along the way. They are going to be used on a daily basis by businesses and a lot of different companies in order to make lots of critical decisions.

For example, medical facilities can use this to help them to help diagnose patients. And we will find that there are a lot of media sites that will rely on machine learning in order to sift through the potential of millions of options in order to give recommendations to the users.

There are many reasons that your business is able to consider using machine learning. For example, it is going to be useful if you are working with a task that is complex or one that is going to involve a larger amount of data and a ton of variables, but there isn't an equation or a formula that is out there right now to handle it. For example, some of the times when we want to work with machine learning include:

1. Equations and rules that are hand-written and too complex to work with. This could include some options like speech recognition and face recognition.

2. When you find that the rules that are going to change all of the time. This could be seen in actions lie fraud detection from a large number of transactional records.

3. ou find that the nature of your data is going to change on a constant basis, and the program has to be able to adapt along the way. This could be seen when we work with predicting the trends during shopping when doing energy demand forecasting and even automated trading, to name a few.

Machine learning is more complex, but we are able to combine it together with Python in order to get some amazing results in the process and to ensure that our data analysis is going to work the way that we want.

How Does Machine Learning Work with Data Analysis?

Now that we understand more about how machine learning works and why it is important, it is time for us to take a look more specifically at how machine learning is able to come in and help us out with our data analysis. There are so many reasons why we are able to use machine learning when it comes to the data analysis, so it is important to take some time to look at how we can use it as well.

Machine learning is basically going to be the underlying process for all of the algorithms that we want to create along the way. No matter how simple or how complex your algorithm will be, a lot of the coding and the mechanics that come with it are going to really be run by the machine learning that we will talk about in this guidebook. And with the help of Python, you can make some really amazing algorithms that help us to sort through the data.

So, if you are actually hoping to go through this process of data analysis with the goal to sort through your data and understand what is found inside of it, then you need to learn a bit about machine learning ahead of time. The good news of this is that machine learning will be able to work well with the Python language we talked about above, making sure we can do it with a simple coding language, even if the ideas that derive from machine learning will be overall more complex.

Supervised Machine Learning

The first type of learning that we need to take a look at here is known as supervised machine learning. This is going to be the most basic form of machine learning that we are able to work with, but it will provide us with some of the different parts that we need in order to keep things going well and can help us to train our algorithms in a quick and efficient manner.

To start, supervised learning is simply going to be the process of helping an algorithm to learn to map an input to a particular output. We are going to spend or time on this one while showing lots of examples, with the corresponding answers, to the algorithm in the hopes that it will find the connections and learn. Then, when the training is done, the algorithm will be able to look at new inputs, without the corresponding output, and give us the right answer on its own.

This whole process is going to be achieved when we work on a labeled data set that was collected earlier. If the mapping is done correctly, the algorithm is going to be able to learn in a successful manner. If it is not reaching the goals here, then that means we have to go through and make some changes to our algorithm to help it learn well. Supervised machine learning algorithms, when they are trained well, will be able to make some good predictions for the new data they get later on in the future.

This is going to be a similar process that we would see with a teacher to student scenario. There is going to be a teacher who is able to guide the student to learn well from books and other materials. The student is then going to be tested and, if they are correct, then the student will pass. If not, then the teacher will change things up and will help the student to learn better, so that they are able to learn from the mistakes that they made in the past so that they get better. This is going to be the basics that come with using supervised machine learning.

Unsupervised Machine Learning

The second type of machine learning that we are able to work with is known as unsupervised learning. This is going to be a method that we can use in data analysis because it will enable the machines to go through and classify both the tangible and intangible objects, without having to go through and provide the machine or the system with any information about of time about the objects.

The things or the objects that our machines are going to need to classify are going to be varied, such as the purchasing behaviors of the customer, some of the patterns of behavior of bacteria, and even things like hacker attacks or fraud happening with a bank. The main idea that we are going to be able to see with this kind of learning is that we want to expose our machines to large volumes of data that are varied and then allowing the algorithm to takes time to learn and infer from the data. However, we need to be able to take the time in order to teach the program how it can learn from that data.

CHAPTER - 7

PYTHON

What is Python, why learn Python?

First, Python is a high-level multi-purpose interpreted language. It is well established and focuses on code readability and ease of use. Furthermore, there are innumerable packages and libraries available for Python, from scientific ones to big data specific. All these libraries, combined with Python's easy learning curve, make this language an incredible tool with great versatility.

Some examples of packages related to Data Analysis and Machine Learning presented in include:

Python

Numpy

Pandas

Scipy

Matplotlib

Seaborn

Bokeh

Scikit-Learn

TensorFlow

Pytorch

These are some of the packages, but many others could be listed.

Additionally, according to <u>Stack Overflow</u>, Python has the largest number of questions when compared to the other major programming languages. This can be shown in the graph below.

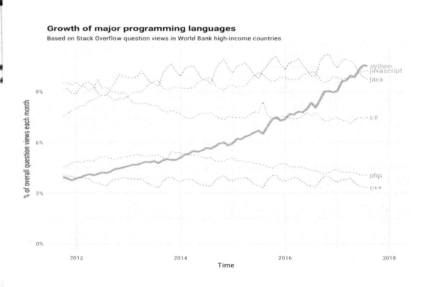

Growth of major programming languages
Based on Stack Overflow question views in World Bank high-income countries

The graph also shows how rapidly this growth happened throughout the years, and that this trend is not slowing down. Therefore, Python is the appropriate language for this book. The version of Python used and referred to in this book is Python 3 because Python 2 is deprecated and soon will not be supported.

Setting Up

1. There are three main ways to download and install Python 3.

   Official Python Website: This installation method is the most common and fastest. However, if you install

Python this way, each external library and packages will have to be installed separately. *Therefore, this method is not recommended.*

2. Miniconda: This installer contains the conda package manager and Python. Once installed, you can use the Anaconda Prompt to install other packages and create environments.

3. Anaconda Distribution: This method includes all the packages used in this book and many others. Therefore, this is the recommended installation process. The downside of this installation is that it requires a large file to be downloaded that may not be ideal, depending on your internet speed and bandwidth restrictions.

In all cases, you should download version 3 of Python, which the most current version and is already widely used and supported by third-party libraries.

Please keep in mind that only one installation process is necessary. You should choose the one that is most adequate for you based on their description above. In general, options 1 and 2 are more appropriate for slow/limited internet connections or low disk space, and option 3 is ideal if there are no internet/ storage restrictions.

Below, there is a small step-by-step installation guide for all the options cited previously.

Download Python from the Official Website

1. On the downloads page of the official Python website https://www.python.org/downloads/, your operating system should be automatically detected and the download option available.

2. If your Operational System is correct, just click on the Download Python Button. Otherwise, select one OS in the options below.

3. After clicking, your download should start right away.

Miniconda

Miniconda

	Windows	Mac OS X	Linux
Python 3.7	64-bit (exe installer)	64-bit (bash installer)	64-bit (bash installer)
	32-bit (exe installer)	64-bit (.pkg installer)	32-bit (bash installer)
Python 2.7	64-bit (exe installer)	64-bit (bash installer)	64-bit (bash installer)
	32-bit (exe installer)	64-bit (.pkg installer)	32-bit (bash installer)

Choose the appropriate OS on the following URL https://docs.conda.io/en/latest/miniconda.html and click on the download button. As always, the download should start, and you can proceed to follow the installation process.

Anaconda Distribution

1. The download section of the Anaconda Distribution for all operating systems is available at https://www.anaconda.com/distribution/#download-section, select your OS.

2. Click Download for version 3, and the download should start right away. Run the installer after the download is completed, and follow the instructions.

Dictionaries

Dictionaries are a powerful data type present in python. It can store indexed values like lists, but the indexes are not a range of integers. Instead, they are unique keys. Therefore, dictionaries are a set of *key: value* pairs. Like sets, dictionaries are not ordered. The keys can be any immutable objects such as strings, tuples, integers, or float numbers.

Defining Dictionaries

Curly brackets and colon are used in an explicit dictionary definition.

```
PYTHON REPL:
>>> a = {}                        # Empty dictionary
>>> a = dict()                    # Empty dictionary
>>> b = {1: 1, 2: 2, 3:3}         # Explicit definitions
>>> c = {42:2, «hi»: 1}
>>> d = {«A»:[1,2,3], «B»: 2}
>>> e = dict(k1=1, k22)           # Considered as string keys
```

Assigning Values to Keys

After a dictionary is created, you can assign values indexing by keys.

```
>>> d = {}                    # Empty dict
>>> d["a"] = [1, 2]           # Assigning list to key "a"
>>> d[2] = "Hello"            # Assigning string to key 2
>>> d
{'a': [1, 2], 2: 'Hello'}
>>> d[2] = «123»              # Overriding value in key 2
>>> d
{'a': [1, 2], 2: '123'}
>>> d[«b»]                    # Access invalid key
KeyError: 'b'
```

Get Keys and Values

Dictionary has the built-in methods keys and values to achieve the current values stored.

```
>>> d = {'a': [1, 2], 2: '123'}    # Same of previous
example
>>> d.keys()                       # List current keys
dict_keys(['a', 2])
>>> d.values()                     # List current values
dict_values([[1, 2], '123'])
```

OBS.: Remember that dictionaries are not an ordered object. Therefore, do not expect order in its keys or values, even though they maintain the insertion order in the latest Python version.

Dictionaries in Loops

In general, you want to know the key: value pairs on a dictionary when iterating. The items method returns both values when used in for loops.

```
INPUT
# Nested Conditions
d = dict(a=1, b=2, c=3)
for k, v in d.items():
print(k)
    print(v)
```

```
OUTPUT
a

1

b

2

c

3
```

Dictionary Comprehension

Dictionaries can be used as in list comprehension.

```
EXAMPLE - Dict Comprehension
# Dict of cubes(values) of number(key) 1 to 4
dc = {x: x ** 3 for x in range(1, 5) }
print(dc)
```

```
OUTPUT
{1: 1, 2: 8, 3: 27, 4: 64}
```

Functions

We already used multiple functions that are built in the Python programming language, such as print, len, or type. Generally, a function is defined to represent a set of instructions that will be repeatedly called. In order to achieve the desired task, a function may or may not need multiple inputs, called arguments.

```
EXAMPLE - Built-in Functions
a = [1, 2, 3]
s = len(a)        # variable a is the argument of function len
print(s)          # variable s is the argument of function
print
OUTPUT
3
```

Not all functions need an argument, for example, the built-in function help.

```
EXAMPLE - Built-in Functions
help()              # no values is passed as argument
OUTPUT
Welcome to Python 3.6's help utility!
...
```

Testing your Code

In a Python programming language, there are several technique methods that are used in testing a particular kind of code. Let us venture into the actual methods that are normally involved:

Automated versus manual testing.

Exploratory testing is a type of manual testing that is committed without a specific plan, where a developer is just trying to explore the actual application. In a bid to complete certain amounts of manual tests, a developer is obligated to draft a list of all the available features that a certain application contains, the various kinds of inputs that are normally accepted, and the possible expected results. With this, the developer is expected to go back to his or her list whenever changes are made to a particular set of programs, an activity that is so much tiresome and unsatisfying. It is at this point where automated testing comes in.

Automated testing is the execution of the set program of code by a script in place of a particular human. Python language comes in handy is a set of tools and certain libraries that aids a particular developer in making automated testing to its application.

Unit tests versus integration tests.

A unit test is basically a kind of smaller test that checks whether a single component in a particular program works the right way so as to make it functional, whereas an integration test is the type of testing that ensures all the components that are involved in a particular set of program work well with each other. Both unit tests and integration tests can be written in a specific program.

Test runners are basically tools that pick up the source code directory of a particular kind of program that contains unit tests and various settings, gets to execute them, and eventually outputs the results to the log files or the console.

CHAPTER - 8

DATA TYPES IN PYTHON

E very program has certain data that allows it to function and operate in the way we want. The data can be a text, a number, or any other thing in between.

Whether complex or as simple as you like, these data types are the cogs in a machine that allow the rest of the mechanism to connect and work.

Python is a host to a few data types and, unlike its competitors, it does not deal with an extensive range of things.

That is good because we have less to worry about and yet achieve accurate results despite the lapse.

Python was created to make our lives, as programmers, a lot easier.

Numeric Data Type

Just as the number suggests, Python is able to recognize numbers rather well.

The numbers are divided into two pairs:

- Integer – A positive and/or negative whole numbers that are represented without any decimal points.
- Float – A real number that has a decimal point representation.

This means, if you were to use 100 and 100.00, one would be identified as an integer while the other will be deemed as a float.

So why do we need to use two various number representations?

If you are designing a program, suppose a small game that has a character's life of 10, you might wish to keep the program in a way that whenever a said character takes a hit, his life reduces by one or two points.

However, to make things a little more precise, you may need to use float numbers.

Now, each hit might vary and may take 1.5, 2.1, or 1.8 points away from the life total.

Using floats allows us to use greater precision, especially when calculations are on the cards.

If you aren't too troubled about the accuracy, or your programming involves whole numbers only, stick to integers.

Booleans

Ah! The one with the funny name.

Boolean (or bool) is a data type that can only operate on and return two values: True or False.

Booleans are a vital part of any program, except the ones where you may never need them, such as our first program.

These are what allow programs to take various paths if the result is true or false.

Here's a little example.

Suppose you are traveling to a country you have never been to.

There are two choices you are most likely to face.

If it is cold, you will be packing your winter clothes.

If it is warm, you will be packing clothes which are appropriate for warm weather.

Simple, right?

That is exactly how the Booleans work.

We will look into the coding aspect of it as well.

For now, just remember, when it comes to true and false, you are dealing with a bool value.

List

While this is slightly more advanced for someone at this stage of learning, the list is a data type that does what it sounds like.

It lists objects, values, or stores data within square brackets ([]).

Here's what a list would look like:

```
month = ['Jan', 'Feb', 'March', 'And so on!']
```

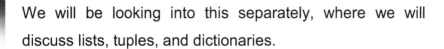

We will be looking into this separately, where we will discuss lists, tuples, and dictionaries.

Surely, they are used within Python, but how?

If you think you can type in the numbers and true and false, all on their own, it will never work.

Variables

You have the passengers, but you do not have a mode of commuting; they will have nowhere to go.

These passengers would just be folks standing around, waiting for some kind of transportation to pick them up.

Similarly, data types cannot function alone.

They need to be 'stored' in these vehicles, which can take them places.

These special vehicles, or as we programmers refer to as containers, are called 'variables,' and they are the elements that perform the magic for us.

Variables are specialized containers that store a specific value in them and can then be accessed, called, modified, or even removed when the need arises.

Every variable that you may create will hold a specific type of data in them.

You cannot add more than one type of data within a variable.

In other programming languages, you will find that in order to create a variable, you need to use the keyword 'var' followed by an equals mark '=' and then the value.

In Python, it is a lot easier, as shown below:

```
name = "John"

age = 33

weight = 131.50

is_married = True
```

In the above, we have created a variable named 'name' and given it a value of characters.

If you recall strings, we have used double quotation marks to let the program know that this is a string.

We then created a variable called age.

Here, we simply wrote 33, which is an integer as there are no decimal figures following that.

You do not need to use quotation marks here at all.

Next, we created a variable 'weight' and assigned it a float value.

Finally, we created a variable called 'is_married' and assigned it a 'True' bool value.

If you were to change the 'T' to 't', the system will not recognize it as a bool and will end up giving an error.

Focus on how we used the naming convention for the last variable.

We will be ensuring that our variables follow the same naming convention.

You can even create blank variables if you feel like you may need these at a later point in time, or wish to initiate them at no value at the start of the application.

For variables with numeric values, you can create a variable with a name of your choosing and assign it a value of zero.

Alternatively, you can create an empty string as well by using opening and closing quotation marks only.

```
empty_variable1 = 0

empty_variable2 = ""
```

You do not have to necessarily name them like this, you can come up with more meaningful names so that you and any other programmer who may read your code would understand.

I have given them these names to ensure anyone can immediately understand their purpose.

Now we have learned how to create variables, let's learn how to call them.

What's the point of having these variables if we are never going to use them, right?

Let's create a new set of variables.

Have a look here:

```
name = "James"

age = 43

height_in_cm = 163

occupation = "Programmer"
```

I do encourage you to use your own values and play around with variables if you like.

In order for us to call the name variable, we simply need to type the name of the variable.

In order to print that to the console, we will do this:

```
print(name)

Output
```

The same goes for the age, the height variable, and occupation.

But what if we wanted to print them together and not separately?

Try running the code below and see what happens:

```
print(name age height_in_cm occupation)
```

Surprised? Did you end up with this?

```
print(name age height_in_cm occupation)
        ^
```

SyntaxError: invalid syntax

Process finished with exit code 1

Here is the reason why that happened.

When you were using a single variable, the program knew what variable that was.

The minute you added a second, a third, and a fourth variable, it tried to look for something that was written in that manner.

Since there wasn't any, it returned with an error that otherwise says:

"Umm… Are you sure, Sir? I tried looking everywhere, but I couldn't find this 'name age height_in_cm occupation' element anywhere."

All you need to do is add a comma to act as a separator like so:

```
print(name, age, height_in_cm, occupation)

Output:

James 43 163 Programmer
```

"Your variables, Sir!"

And now, it knew what we were talking about.

The system recalled these variables and was successfully able to show us what their values were.

But what happens if you try to add two strings together?

What if you wish to merge two separate strings and create a third-string as a result?

```
first_name = "John"

last_name = "Wick"
```

To join these two strings into one, we can use the '+' sign.

The resulting string will now be called a String Object, and since this is Python we are dealing with, everything within this language is considered as an object.

```
first_name = "John"

last_name = "Wick"

first_name + last_name
```

Here, we did not ask the program to print the two strings.

If you wish to print these two instead, simply add the print function and type in the string variables with a + sign in the middle within parentheses.

Sounds good, but the result will not be quite what you expect:

```
first_name = "John"

last_name = "Wick"

print(first_name + last_name)

Output:

JohnWick
```

Hmm. Why do you think that happened?

Certainly, we did use a space between the two variables.

The problem is that the two strings have combined together, quite literally here, and we did not provide a white space (blank space) after John or before Wick; it will not include that.

Even the white space can be a part of a string.

To test it out, add one character of space within the first line of code by tapping on the friendly spacebar after John.

Now try running the same command again, and you should see "John Wick" as your result.

The process of merging two strings is called concatenation.

While you can concatenate as many strings as you like, you cannot concatenate a string and an integer together.

If you really need to do that, you will need to use another technique to convert the integer into a string first and then concatenate the same.

CHAPTER - 9

OBJECT ORIENTED PROGRAMMING

IN PYTHON

Object and Class in Python

Python supports different programming approaches as it is a multi-paradigm. An object in Python has an attribute and behavior.

Example

Car as an object:

Attributes: color, mileage, model, age.

Behavior: reverse, speed, turn, roll, stop, start.

Class

It is a template for creating an object.

Example

class Car:

NOTE:

By convention, we write the class name with the first letter as uppercase. A class name is in singular form by convention.

Syntax
class Name_of_Class:

From a class, we can construct objects by simply making an instance of the class. The class_name() operator creates an object by assigning the object to the empty method.

Object/Class Instantiation

From our class Car, we can have several objects such as a first car, second care or SUVs.

Example

Start IDLE.

Navigate to the File menu and click New Window.

Type the following:

```
my_car=Car()
```

   pass

Practice Exercise

Create a class and an object for students.

Create a class and an object for the hospital.

Create a class and an object for a bank.

Create a class and an object for a police department.

Example

Start IDLE.

Navigate to the File menu and click New Window.

Type the following:

```
class Car:

category="Personal Automobile"

    def __init__(self, model, insurance):

        self.model = model

        self.insurance =insurance

subaru=Car("Subaru","Insured")

toyota=Car("Toyota","Uninsured")

print("Subaru is a {}".format(subaru._class_.car))

print("Toyota is a {}".format(toyota._class_.car))

print("{} is {}".format(subaru.model, subaru.insurance))

print("{} is {}".format(toyota.model, toyota.insurance))
```

Methods

Functions defined within a body of the class are known as methods and are basic functions. Methods define the behaviors of an object.

Example

Start IDLE.

Navigate to the File menu and click New Window.

Type the following:

```
def __init__(self, model, insurance):

    self.model = model

    self.insurance =insurance

  def ignite(self, ignite):

    return "{} ignites {}".format(self.model, ignition)

  def stop(self):

    return "{} is now stopping".format(self.model)

subaru=Car("Subaru","Insured")

print(subaru.ignite("'Fast'"))

print(subaru.stop())
```

NOTE

The methods ignite() and stop() are referred to as instance methods because they are an instance of the object created.

Practice Exercise

- Create a class Dog and instantiate it.
- Create a Python program to show names of two dogs and their two attributes from a.

Inheritance

A way of creating a new class by using details of existing class devoid of modifying it is called inheritance. The derived class or child class is the newly formed class while the existing class is called parent or base class.

Example

Start IDLE.

Navigate to the File menu and click New Window.

Type the following:

```python
class Dog:

    def __init__(self):

        print("Dog is available")

    def whoisThis(self):

        print("Dog")

    def walk(self):

        print("Walks gently")

class Spitz(Dog):        #Child class

    def __init__(self):

        super().__init__()

        print("Spitz is now available")
```

```
    def whoisThis(self):

        print("Pitbull")

    def wag(self):

        print("Strong")

pitbull = Pitbull()

pitbull.whoisThis()

pitbull.walk()

pitbull.wag()
```

Discussion

We created two Python classes in the program above. The classes were Dog as the base class and Pitbull as the derived class. The derived class inherits the functions of the base class. The method _init_() and the function super() are used to pull the content of _init_() method from the base class into the derived class.

Encapsulation in Python

Encapsulation in Python Object Oriented Programming approach is meant to help prevent data from direct modification. Private attributes in Python are denoted using a single or double underscore as a prefix.

Example

Start IDLE.

Navigate to the File menu and click New Window.

Type the following:

"__" or "_".

```python
class Tv:
    def __init__(self):
        self.__Finalprice = 800
    def offer(self):
        print("Offering Price: {}".format(self.__finalprice))
    def set_final_price(self, offer):
        self.__finalprice = offer
t = Tv()
t.offer()
t.__finalprice = 950
t.offer()
# using setter function
t.setFinalPrice(990)
t.sell()
```

Discussion

The program defined a class Tv and used _init_(0 methods to hold the final offering price of the TV. Along the way, we attempted to change the price but could not manage. The reason for the inability to change is because Python treated the _finalprice as private attributes. The only way to modify this value was through using a setter function, setMaxPrice() that takes price as a parameter.

Object Creation in Python

Example from the previous class

Open the previous program file with class Bright

```
student1=Bright ()
```

Discussion

The last program will create object student1, a new instance. The attributes of objects can be accessed via the specific object name prefix. The attributes can be a method or data including the matching class functions. In other terms, Bright.salute is a function object and student1.salute will be a method object.

```
Example

Start IDLE.

Navigate to the File menu and click New Window.
```

Type the following:

```
class Bright:

    "Another class again!"

    c = 20

    def salute(self):

        print('Hello')

student2 = Bright()

print(Bright.salute)

print(student2.salute)

student2.salute()
```

Discussion

We invoked the student2.salute() despite the parameter 'self' and it still worked without placing arguments. The reason for this phenomenon is because each time an object calls its method, the object itself is passed as the first argument. The implication is that student2.salute() translates into student2.salute(student2). It is the reason for the 'self; name.

Constructors

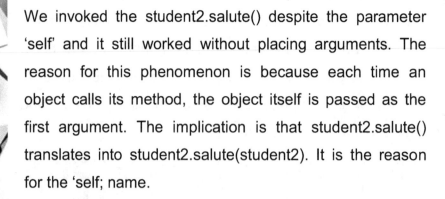

Start IDLE.

Navigate to the File menu and click New Window.

Type the following:

```
class NumberComplex

class ComplexNumber:

    def __init__(self,realnum = 0,i = 0):

        self.real = realnum

        self.imaginarynum = i

    def getData(self):

        print("{0}+{1}j".format(self.realnumber,self.imaginarynum))

complex1 = NumberComplex(2,3)

complex1.getData()

complex2 = NumberComplex(5)

complex2.attribute = 10

print((complex2.realnumber,

complex2.imaginarynumber, complex2.attribute))

complex1.attribute
```

Deleting Objects and Attributes

- The del statement is used to delete attributes of an object at any instance.

Example

Start IDLE.

Navigate to the File menu and click New Window.

Type the following:

complex1 = NumberComplex(2,3)

del complex1.imaginarynumber

complex1.getData()

del NumberComplex.getData

complex1.getData()

Deleting the Entire Object

Example

Start IDLE.

Navigate to the File menu and click New Window.

Type the following:

complex1=NumberComplex (1,3)

del complex1

Discussion

When complex1=NumberComplex(1,3) is done, a new instance of the object gets generated in memory and the name complex1 ties with it. The object does not immediately get destroyed as it temporarily stays in memory before the garbage collector purges it from memory. The purging of the object helps free resources bound to the object and enhances system efficiency. Garbage destruction Python refers to automatic destruction of unreferenced objects.

Inheritance in Python

In Python inheritance allows us to specify a class that takes all the functionality from the base class and adds more. It is a powerful feature of OOP.

Syntax

class ParentClass:

  Body of parent class

class ChildClass(ParentClass):

  Body of derived class

Example

Start IDLE.

Navigate to the File menu and click New Window.

Type the following:

```
class Rect_mine(Rect_mine):

   def __init__(self):

      Shape.__init__(self,4)

   def getArea(self):

      s1, s2, s3,s4 = self.count_sides

      perimeter = (s1+s2+s3+s4)

      area = (s1*s2)

      print('The rectangle area is:' %area)
```

Example 2

```
r = rect_mine()

r.inputSides()
```

Type b1 : 4

Type l1 : 8

Type b2 : 4

Type l1:   8

r.dispSides()

Type b1 is 4.0

Type l1 is 8.0

```
Type b2 is 4.0

Type l1 is 8.0

r.getArea()
```

Method Overriding in Python

When a method is defined in both the base class and the
derived class, the method in the child class/derived class
will override the parent/base class. In the above example,
init() method in Rectangle class will override the _init_()
in Shape class.

Inheritance in Multiple Form in Python

Example

Start IDLE.

Navigate to the File menu and click New Window.

Type the following:

```
class Parent1:

    pass

class Parent2:

    pass

class MultiInherit(Parent1, Parent2):
```

```
    pass
```

In this case, MultiInherit is derived from class Parent1 and Parent2.

Multilevel Inheritance

Inheriting from a derived class is called multilevel inheritance.

Example

Start IDLE.

Navigate to the File menu and click New Window.

Type the following:

```
class Parent:

    pass

class Multilevel1(Parent):

    pass

class Multilevel2(Multilevel1):

    pass
```

Discussion

Multilevel1 derives from Parent, and Multilevel2 derives from Multilevel1.

Method Resolution Order

Example

Start IDLE.

Navigate to the File menu and click New Window.

Type the following:

```
print(issubclass(list,object))

print(isinstance(6.7,object))

print(isinstance("Welcome",object))
```

Discussion

The particular attribute in a class will be scanned first. The search will continue into parent classes. This search does not repeat searching the same class twice. The approach or order of searching is sometimes called linearization of multiderived class in Python. The Method Resolution Order refers to the rules needed to determine this order.

Operator Overloading

Inbuilt classes can use operators and the same operators will behave differently with different types. An example is the + that depending on context will perform concatenation

of two strings, arithmetic addition on numbers, or merge lists. Operating overloading is an OOP feature that allows assigning varying meaning to an operator subject to context.

Making Class Compatible with Inbuilt Special Functions

Example

Start IDLE.

Navigate to the File menu and click New Window.

Type the following:

```
class Planar:

    def __init__(self, x_axis= 0, y_axis = 0):

        self.x_axis = x_axis

        self.y_axis = y_axis

    def __str__(self):

        return "({0},{1})".format(self.x_axis,self.y_axis)
```

Discussion

```
planar1=Planar(3,5)

print(planar1)          #The output will be (3,5)
```

Using More Inbuilt Methods

Example

Start IDLE.

Navigate to the File menu and click New Window.

Type the following:

```
class Planar:

    def __init__(self, x_axis= 0, y_axis = 0):

        self.x_axis = x_axis

        self.y_axis = y_axis

str(planar1)

format(planar1)
```

Discussion

It then follows that each time we invoke format(planar1) or str(planar1), Python is in effect executing planar1._str_() thus the name, special functions.

CHAPTER - 10

LEARNING PYTHON FROM SCRATCH

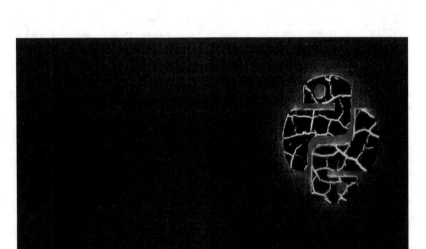

E ven before buying this book, you had some idea as to how important and in-demand Python is. We also read a little about it earlier on and saw how it is overtaking many mainstream programming languages. We walked through a step-by-step guide to download Python 3, the integrated development environment, or the text/code editor and set everything up. Lastly, you created your first program: well done!

Now, it is time to stop scratching the surface and dive deep into the world of Python. There are far too many components and aspects to learn about Python, but we will only be focusing on what is essential for anyone to know and learn as a beginner.

Consider this as a grammar for any other language. Without grammar, the language sounds broken, and so does Python.

Python at First Glance

Let us start with the program below:

```python
print("I made it!")

print("======")

print("If I only knew it would be this easy")

print("======")

print("I would have taken up Python ages ago")

print("======")
```

We used a print command to have our message printed at the console box as our output of the program. Calling 'print' a command is technically wrong; it is a function.

While we will be covering functions and methods in detail later on, for now, just remember that functions are names of commands which are followed by parenthesis "()" where the brackets will either be empty or contain some type of data. There are set parameters that are pre-defined, meaning that certain functions will only be able to accept a specific type of data.

In the above example, we used nothing more than text. A few letters to create a message, and that is it. In Python, things work differently. Text is not identified as text. We need to tell Python that we want this to be printed as text. How do we do that? We use single or double quotation marks, which allows Python to understand that anything within the quotes is text, and it needs to print it the way it is.

I bet you most of you may not have noticed how all of the lines start with a lowercase 'p' instead of the opposite. Ah, yes! Now that you noticed it let me tell you why we did that.

Python is a case-sensitive language. It considers everything as a character, not a letter or text. This means that the lowercase 'p' will not be the same character as the uppercase 'P' and so on, and so forth.

Print

PRINT

print

PrinT

pRINt

All of these will be treated differently by Python, and for printing purposes, these will not work at all except for 'print' as that is the standard way of outputting things.

To name anything in Python, we normally use lowercases for one-word commands. This isn't something that is exclusive to Python, as every language uses some way as standard to write codes. What makes Python different is the sheer amount of thought that was put into the naming convention to make code easier to read. Remember this, anything with more than the word, you can use a few ways to do so as shown here:

last_name

LastName

lastname

LASTNAME

In most of the cases, we will be using the first approach where each letter begins with a lowercase. For components with more than one word, we will be using underscores to separate them. The next in line is generally used only in cases of classes. At this point in time, you do not have to worry about what classes are. Just remember that words with the first letter as capital and that having no underscores is an example of Camel Case, and used for classes.

Next down the line is the way we use to name packages. Here, all the words begin and end with lowercase letters and have no underscores between them. On the polar opposite, we have our last entry, which is used to define constants. Here, all the letters are in uppercase and have no underscores separating the words.

Boring, wasn't it? I know! But it is something you may want to remember as we will be doing quite a lot of these. You should know when to use which convention, as this greatly improves the code readability. The entire point of Python is to promote code readability, and if we go against that, there's not much point in learning Python.

Now that we have covered this let us start by discussing data types that are at work within Python. Without these, no programming language would operate or work. They are what we use as inputs, and these are what direct the program per our desire accordingly.

What Are Data Types?

Every program has certain data that allows it to function and operate in the way we want. The data can be a text, a number, or any other thing in between. Whether complex in nature or as simple as you like, these data types are the cogs in a machine that allow the rest of the mechanism to connect and work.

Python is a host to a few data types and, unlike its competitors, it does not deal with an extensive range of things. That is good because we have less to worry about and yet achieve accurate results despite the lapse. Python was created to make our lives, as programmers, a lot easier.

Strings

In Python, and other programming languages, any text value that we may use, such as names, places, sentences, they are all referred to as strings. A string is a collection of characters, not words or letters, which is marked by the use of single or double quotation marks.

To display a string, use the print command, open up a parenthesis, put in a quotation mark, and write anything. Once done, we generally end the quotation marks and close the bracket.

Since we are using PyCharm, the IntelliSense detects what we are about to do and delivers the rest for us

immediately. You may have noticed how it jumped to the rescue when you only type in the opening bracket. It will automatically provide you with a closing one. Similarly, for the quotation marks, one or two, it will provide the closing ones for you. See why we are using PyCharm? It greatly helps us out.

"I do have a question. Why do we use either single or double quotation marks if both provide the same result?"

Ah! Quite the eye. There is a reason we use these, let me explain by using the example below:

```
print('I'm afraid I won't be able to make it')

print("He said "Why do you care?"")
```

Try and run this through PyCharm. Remember, to run, simply click on the green play-like button on the top right side of the interface.

"C:\Users\Programmer\AppData\Local\Programs\Python\Python37-32\python.exe"
"C:/Users/Programmer/PycharmProjects/PFB/Test1.py"

File
"C:/Users/Programmer/PycharmProjects/PFB/Test1.py",
line 1

```
print('I'm afraid I won't be able to make it')
```

SyntaxError: invalid syntax

Process finished with exit code 1

Here's a hint: That's an error!

So what happened here? Try and revisit the inputs. See how we started the first print statement with a single quote? Immediately, we ended the quote using another quotation mark. The program only accepted the letter 'I' as a string. You may have noticed how the color may have changed for every other character from 'm' until 'won' after which the program detects yet another quotation mark and accepts the rest as another string. Quite confusing, to be honest.

Similarly, in the second statement, the same thing happened. The program saw double quotes and understood it as a string, right until the point the second instance of double quotation marks arrives. That's where it did not bother checking whether it is a sentence or that it may have still been going on. Computers do not understand English; they understand binary communications. The compiler is what runs when we press the run button. It compiles our code and interprets the same into a series of ones and zeros so that the computer may understand what we are asking it to do.

This is exactly why the second it spots the first quotation mark, it considers it as a start of a string, and ends it immediately when it spots a second quotation mark, even if the sentence was carrying onwards.

To overcome this obstacle, we use a mixture of single and double quotes when we know we need to use one of these within the sentence. Try and replace the opening and closing quotation marks in the first state as double quotation marks on both ends. Likewise, change the quotation marks for the second statement to single quotation marks as shown here:

```
print("I'm afraid I won't be able to make it")

print('He said "Why do you care?"')
```

Now the output should look like this:

I'm afraid I won't be able to make it

He said "Why do you care?"

Lastly, for strings, the naming convention does not apply to the text of the string itself. You can use regular English writing methods and conventions without worries, as long as that is within the quotation marks. Anything outside it will not be a string in the first place, and will or may not work if you change the cases.

Did you know that strings also use triple quotes? Never heard that before, have you? We will cover that shortly!

Numeric Data type

Just as the number suggests, Python is able to recognize numbers rather well. The numbers are divided into two pairs:

- Integer – A positive and/or negative whole numbers that are represented without any decimal points.
- Float – A real number that has a decimal point representation.

This means, if you were to use 100 and 100.00, one would be identified as an integer while the other will be deemed as a float. So why do we need to use two various number representations?

If you are designing a program, suppose a small game that has a character's life of 10, you might wish to keep the program in a way that whenever a said character takes a hit, his life reduces by one or two points. However, to make things a little more precise, you may need to use float numbers. Now, each hit might vary and may take 1.5, 2.1, or 1.8 points away from the life total.

Using floats allows us to use greater precision, especially when calculations are on the cards. If you aren't too troubled about the accuracy, or your programming involves whole numbers only, stick to integers.

CHAPTER - 11

TOP PROGRAMMING LANGUAGES AT TOP COMPANIES AND PYTHON

Python is consistently contrasted and other deciphered dialects, for example, Java, JavaScript, Perl, Tcl, or Smalltalk. Associations with C++,

Common Lisp and Scheme can likewise be edifying. Around there, I will rapidly contrast Python and all of these dialects. These examinations center around what every language gives in a manner of speaking. The decision of a programming language is a significant part of the time composed by other legitimate impediments, for instance, cost, accessibility, getting ready, and prior endeavor, or even enthusiastic connection. Since these perspectives are exceptionally factor, it has all the earmarks of being a pointless activity to consider them much for this relationship.

Java

Python programs are usually expected to run more gradually than Java programs, yet they likewise put aside generously less exertion to create. Python programs are normally 3-5 times shorter than indistinguishable Java programs. This distinction can be credited to Python's worked unimportant level data types and its dynamic forming. For example, a Python programming engineer consumes no time pronouncing the sorts of factors or contentions, and Python's amazing polymorphic rundown. Moreover, word reference types, for which rich syntactic help are gotten straight together with the language, discover use in essentially every Python program. Because of the run-time composing, Python's run time must perform progressively intensive contrasted with Java programming language. For example, while assessing the articulation a+b, it ought to at first research the things on a and b to discover their type, which isn't known at compile time. It by then gathers the reasonable expansion activity, which may be an over-burden client characterized technique. Java, on the other hand, can play out a successful number or skimming point expansion, in any case, requires variable assertions for an and b, and doesn't permit over-burdening of the + administrator for events of client characterized classes.

Consequently, Python is an unfathomably improved fit as a "stick" language, while Java is better portrayed as a low-level usage language. Truly, the two together make a splendid blend. Parts can be made in Java and united to shape applications in Python; Python can likewise be utilized to show sections until their game plan can be "solidified" in a Java execution. To assist this with arranging of progress, a Python usage written in Java is a work in progress, which permits calling Python code from Java and the contrary path around. In this use, Python source code is suggested Java bytecode (with assistance from a run-time library to help Python's dynamic semantics).

JavaScript

Python's "object-based" subset is commonly proportionate to JavaScript. Like JavaScript (and not in any manner like Java), Python bolsters a programming style that uses basic capacities and factors without partaking in class definitions. Python, obviously, underpins composing a lot greater ventures and better code reuse through a genuine article situated programming style, where classes and legacy accept a huge job.

Perl

Python and Perl begin from a comparative foundation (UNIX scripting, which both have long grown out of), and sport various comparative highlights, yet have a substitute method of working. Perl accentuates support for fundamental application-situated errands, for instance, by having worked in standard articulations, document filtering and report making highlights. Python accentuates support for ordinary programming strategies, for instance, data structure plan and article arranged programming, and urges programming architects to compose clear (and along these lines practical) code by giving a rich anyway not excessively mysterious documentation. As a result, Python approaches Perl yet rarely beats it in its unique application area; in any case, Python has importance well past Perl's forte.

Tcl

Like Python, Tcl is commonsense as an application development language, just as an autonomous programming language. Notwithstanding, Tcl, which for the most part stores all data as strings, is weak on data structures and executes normal code much more slow than Python. Tcl likewise needs includes required for composing tremendous endeavors, for example, explicit namespaces. All things considered, while a "standard" gigantic application using Tcl usually contains Tcl increases recorded in C or C++ that are obvious to that application, a comparable Python application can much of the time be written in "unadulterated Python". Unadulterated Python improvement is much quicker than to compose and investigate a C or C++ programming language part. It has been said that Tcl's one sparing worth is the Tk toolbox. Python has gotten an interface to Tk as its standard GUI part library.

cl 8.0 keeps an eye on the speed issues by giving a bytecode compiler limited data type backing, besides, it fuses namespaces. In any case, it is uptil now an on a very basic level progressively bulky programming language.

Smalltalk

Perhaps the most noteworthy distinction among Python and Smalltalk is Python's more "standard" grammar, which gives up it a leg on engineer planning. Like Smalltalk, Python has dynamic and obligatory composition, and everything in Python is a thing. Smalltalk's standard library of variety data types is progressively refined, while Python's library has more workplaces for overseeing Internet and WWW genuine components, for instance, email, HTML and FTP.

Python has an alternate method of working concerning the improved condition and circulation of code. Where Smalltalk by and large has a solid "system picture" which contains both the earth and the client's program, Python stores both standard modules and client modules in particular documents which can without a very remarkable stretch be redone or conveyed outside the structure. One outcome is that there is numerous decision for connecting a Graphical User Interface (GUI) to a Python program since the GUI isn't solidified with the structure.

C++

Practically totally said for Java additionally applies for C++, just more so: where Python code is normally 3-5 times shorter than proportionate Java code, it is much of the time 5-10 times shorter than equivalent C++ code! Story confirmation suggests that one Python programming architect can finish in two months what two C++ engineers can't complete in a year. Python sparkles as a paste language used to consolidate parts written in C++.

Basic Lisp and Scheme

These dialects are close to Python in their dynamic semantics, yet so phenomenal in their way to deal with sentence structure that an examination turns out to be just about a strict contention: is Lisp's absence of grammar a touch of a bit of leeway or a hindrance? It ought to be seen that Python has careful cutoff points like those of Lisp, and Python exercises can create and execute program parts on the fly. Typically, genuine properties are authoritative: Common Lisp is enormous (in each sense), and the Scheme world is partitioned between various contradictory adaptations, where Python has a solitary, free, minimal execution.

CHAPTER - 12

WEB AND DESKTOP APP

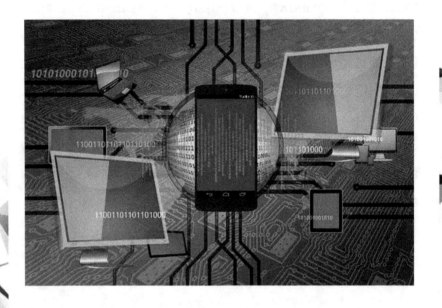

An internet software runs on a far off server as a software program utility. Most of the time, web browsers are for net packages like the net. Some of the packages are used for intranets, schools, firms, and organizations. They are not the same as other applications since you do now not want to put in them. Some of the not unusual net packages consist of Flickr, Wikipedia, Facebook, and Mibbit. They are famous due to the fact that maximum of the running systems is on the net browser and programmers can exchange them with ease.

Several blessings come with the use of internet software:

They do no longer want to be mounted due to the fact they run internal a browser. They do no longer require numerous space for storage handiest a display of facts.

- With internet packages. It helps with compatibility problems; all is wanted is a browser.

- Most of the records used are remotely stored; for this reason, ease of cooperation and communication.

- Web software enables in mail and communication.

Apart from the listed blessings of web packages, there also are drawbacks:

Most of the recognized internet packages will seem to look special in comparison to the normal applications. The purpose is that they run inside a browser. The person experience might be extraordinary and no longer appreciated via many.

To be capable of observing standards, web packages want to be coded, and any small modifications will prevent the internet software from being used in any browser.

There is a need to have a connection among the web software and the server so as for it to run smoothly. For the connection to happen, you will need bandwidth. And when the connection isn't always adequate, you can experience facts loss or the utility could be usable.

Most of the internet programs rely upon the server that hosts them. When it's far off, the net software isn't always usable, however the conventional applications will still paintings.

The overall control of the net utility is with the mother employer. They have the strength to create a new version while they experience like it.

When the data is remotely stored, exporting it to be used by other programs might be hard.

Web applications permit the organization to track all of the activities of the users, therefore private issues.

At this point, you need to recognize how an internet application works. Most of the internet programs are coded in a language this is browser supported, like HTML or JavaScript. And the foremost purpose is that the languages rely on the browser to be able to execute their programs. You need to recognize that a number of these packages are dynamic, and they'll require server-aspect processing. Others are considered static and will now not want any processing from the server.

When you have an internet software, you will want a webserver to manage all of the requests that the customer has. The server will assist in performing all the obligations and store records and statistics. The software server consists of ASP, PHP, and JSP. A normal web utility has a specific flow:

The user will trigger a request the usage of the internet that is going to the webserver. This may be done through the web browser or consumer interface at the application.

The web server will then ahead that request to the unique web application server.

The asked project might be performed through the internet utility server; this includes querying the database or information processing with the intention to generate the specified results.

The results will be dispatched to the internet server by way of of the net application server; that is in regards to the statistics processed or the specified data.

The client gets a response from the webserver; they'll get the information that they have got requested and it will seem on the user's display.

There are numerous examples of net applications which includes buying carts, phrase processors, on line forms, document conversions, and scanning, on line forms, and e-mail applications like Yahoo and Gmail.

How to Work with Django

Django is used to create net programs. It is in particular meant to create a web software that connects to a database. You can also cope with consumer management, properly security, and internationalization. Some of the commonplace net packages include Disqus, Pinterest, and Instagram. You can use Django as standalone libraries although it will require extra work. That is the purpose why it isn't always really useful to use it as a standalone.

Django is a mixture of one-of-a-kind components that paintings via responding to user requests.

The first step is the request-or-reaction machine. The predominant paintings are to get hold of and return web responses. Django will accept all the requests of the URLs and return all the HTML facts to the internet browser. The page may be in simple textual content or something better.

The internet requests will enter the Django software through the

URLs. The simplest entry point for any Django utility is the URLs; developers have the manipulate of the to be had URLs. When you access the URL, Django will permit the viewing.

All your requests might be processed by using the views. Django perspectives are considered to be codes generated from Python when the URL is accessed. Views are something easy like returning a text to the consumer. The textual content may be made complex. It can be form processing, credit score card processing, and database querying. When the view has finished processing, an internet response is sent to the consumer. When net response is returned, the user can get admission to the URL at the browser they will get entry to the response. This might be an HTML net page that indicates a mixture of photos and text, and they are created using the templating system from Django. With Django facts, there's flexibility to have extra packages. You can use which you create an easy blog, cell applications, or a desktop. Django framework is powered by way of web sites like Instagram and Pinterest.

User Accounts

A user account is at the community server that is used to save the username of the computer, password, and any applicable statistics. When you have got the user account, it will permit you or no longer to connect to other computers or networks. With a network with a couple of users, you will want person accounts. A correct example of a user account is your e-mail account.

There are extraordinary styles of person money owed, irrespective of the working device that you are using. You may be capable of trace, authenticate, and monitor all the services. When you put in a running device, it creates user bills to have get admission to after the installation. After the installation, you'll have four consumer accounts; device account, outstanding consumer account, normal and visitor person account.

System account: These are accounts that might be used to get admission to resources in the system. The running system will use these accounts to know if a service is allowed to get entry to the assets or now not. When they are established, they invent relevant accounts; and after installation, the account might be capable of get admission to the needed information. If you are a network or machine administrator, you may not want to have any information approximately the debts.

Super user account: This account is privileged within the working device. When one is the use of Windows, the account is referred to as the Administrator account. When the use of Linux, the account is the basis account, and the working gadget will assist the user entire one-of-a-kind responsibilities. Tasks are like beginning services, developing and deleting new consumer accounts, putting in new software program, and changing system documents.

Regular user account: This account does not have many privileges and cannot make modifications within the device homes and files. They simplest function on obligations that they're authorized like going for walks applications, developing files, and customizing variables.

The Guest person account: This is the account that has less privilege; you will no longer be capable of change something with the gadget. The account is understood to perform temporary responsibilities like playing games, watching movies, or surfing the net. Using Windows, this account may be created after installation; and in Linux, you may need to create the account manually after installation.

The subsequent step is to recognize a way to create a person account. When you've got a couple of users the usage of the same computer, you may want to have new person money owed for every person. When using

Windows, you may create several debts. Each of the person bills has its very own settings. It will assist you to manipulate the documents separately, and when every user logs in, it will likely be like their very own computer.

The first step in growing a person account is to click on START on the CONTROL PANEL then click on ADD or REMOVE person money owed. Click on CREATE A NEW ACCOUNT and select the account type. You will enter the account name after which choose the account type which you desire to create. The administrator has the privilege to create and alternate accounts and putting in applications. The distinction is a popular user can't perform such tasks. The closing step might be to click at the CREATE ACCOUNT button and close the CONTROL PANEL.

How to Style and Deploy an App

There are special deployment options that want to be taken into consideration. When an app is developed in the utility builder, it is created within the workplace. All the places of work have IDs and names; all you need is to create a software within the improvement and then installation it in production.

During deployment, you will decide wherein you want the existing ID to be inside the workplace, current HTTP server, or in growing new ones. The deployment options encompass.

You will first create a software this is expressed with the aid of quit-users.

The fine manner to installation a software is by growing an Application Express for stop users. Then sent the URL and login information to the users. It will work whilst the consumer population is tolerant and small.

You will need to apply the equal schema and workplace. You want to export after which import the utility, then set up that underneath a different application ID. This method will work whilst there are fewer adjustments to any known objects.

Use the equal schema and a different workplace, export all, after which import the applications into every other workplace. It will prevent any production and modification with the aid of developers.

Use a one of a kind schema and workspace. Export after which import the software right into a separate workplace, and install it in a separate schema.

Use an exclusive database for all variations. Export then import to another oracle utility and then deploy it to a distinctive database and schema.

To set up an app, within the configuration supervisor console, click on SOFTWARE LIBRARY. Go to APPLICATION MANAGEMENT after which select APPLICATION or APPLICATION GROUP.

Choose from a utility or software group from the install listing and click on DEPLOY.

CHAPTER - 13

PROJECTS

Project - 1 (Game)

Before I provide you with your first project, let me quickly shed some light on what you can expect from these projects.

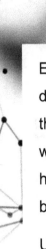

Every project will be unique, as each one of us will have different ideas about how to carry out the task and execute the same. The projects will be designed to provide you with seemingly simple tasks, only to find out that you may have to do a little more than just copying and pasting blocks of code from one file to another.

Use your coding knowledge from all sources, as these will not be bound to individual chapters. Projects are where you will encounter all kinds of problems, situations, and scenarios. To solve these, or finish them successfully, you will need to use various methods right from the beginning, all the way to the end of complex matters like functions, classes, and modules.

I will be providing you with links from which you can download specific modules, libraries, or classes to help further make the process easier. You already know how to import them into your PyCharm using the "from x import y" or "import xyz" method. Try and make a simple-looking scenario complex and interesting. Continue developing these projects with advanced knowledge that you will hopefully gain after this book. A program is never truly complete. Even the best programs and software continue to be updated with newer knowledge, modules, and variations.

Keep on practicing and adding more to these projects. Who knows, you might end up with something far superior and more useful than just a message that says "Hello World" at the end.

Task:

Create a simple game of "Rock, Paper, Scissors," where the computer randomly generates value and asks the user to input their selection. The result should show whether the user wins or loses, or if it is a draw.

Requirements:

To complete this project, you will need to use the following:

Packages:

From random import randint – This will be your first line of code. Random comes pre-installed and allows you to force the computer to randomize the selection. This will help you in ensuring that every turn is unique and unpredictable.

There are quite a few ways you can complete this project. As a reference, I will share my solution for this project at the end of the book as well.

Please note that I wish to encourage you to explore the world of Python and use your genuine approaches, communicate with the community, and learn better ways to code. For this reason, I will not share the details on the

projects moving forward. I will gladly share the answers to questions and solutions to other problems. The rest, I invite you to use your power of deduction and programming to learn better.

So far, we have gone through some exercises, questioned what was right and what was not. We even initiated our very first project, which is quite challenging in all fairness. However, everything hinges on how well you understand your basics. The better you know them, the easier it will be to move from a beginner to an intermediate programmer and eventually to a skilled programmer. If you are unsure about certain aspects, it is always a good habit to revisit the concepts and revise what you have learned.

Time to say goodbye to variables and storing values and move on to our friends, the statements, and loops.

Project - 2

Time for yet another project. Since we are discussing games, create a Python program that lets the user know their astrological sign from the given date of birth. The program may seem rather easy, but once you look into the smaller details, you will soon realize that this will require you to think a little out of the box.

For this project, I will not be providing hints nor a model to follow. You already know, and you should be able to execute this one with ease and a bit of finesse as well. You do not need any special modules or packages to get this project done. All you need is a quick search on the internet to see which star sign starts when to get you going.

Through trial and error, you should be able to create a program that can work easily and exceptionally. Should you encounter issues, try and resolve them on your own instead of looking for a solution on the internet.

If such projects interest you, you can find many more by searching for "Python projects for beginners" and get started. The more projects you work on, the better you will learn. Keep an eye out for what is in demand these days and set your target to one day be able to carry out programming of a level that will get you paid handsomely.

CONCLUSION

Thank you for making it to the end of Python Crash Course. Let us hope that it was informative and able to provide you with all of the tools you need to achieve your goals whatever they may be. The objective of this is to present an introduction for the absolute beginners to machine learning and data science.

This covers the dominant machine learning paradigms, namely supervised, unsupervised, semi-supervised, and reinforcement. This explains how to develop machine learning models in general and how to develop a neural network which is a particular method of performing machine learning. It teaches how to train and evaluate their accuracy.

Python is a widely used programming language for different applications and in particular for machine learning. This covers the basic Python programming as well as a guide to use Python libraries for machine learning.

This presents machine learning applications using real datasets to help you enhance your Python programming skills as well as machine learning basics acquired through the book. These applications provide examples of developing a machine learning model for predictions using linear regression, a classifier using logistic regression and artificial neural network. Through these applications, examples of data exploration and visualization using Python are presented.

Nowadays, machine learning is used in every domain, such as marketing, health care systems, banking systems, stock market, gaming applications, among others. This book's objective is to provide a basic understanding of the significant branches of machine learning as well as the philosophy behind artificial neural networks. This also aims at providing Python programming skills for machine learning to beginners with no earlier programming skills in Python or any other programming language.

Remember that deep learning is relatively easy, contrary to collective thinking among programmers. The industry is quickly moving toward the top to take control of machines. There are lots of people who are firmly in favor of machine learning, but I have some solid reasons that deep learning is more profitable than machine learning. Practically speaking, deep learning is a subset of machine learning. It secures power and flexibility by learning the world on the basis of the database that it has stored in the backend.

It works on the back of its hidden learning architecture that consists of multiple layers with some dense layers. The data is processed through these layers where the neural networks get to work on matching the input data with the data that is stored in the databases in the backend. Upon each match, they return the output on the basis of some highly educated findings that are efficient and very well managed.

Once you have acquired the skills and understood the reasoning behind machine learning models presented in this book, you will be able to use these skills to solve complex problems using machine learning. You will also be able to easily acquire other skills and use more advanced machine learning methods. In this guide, I explained to you the basics of Python language. Learning to program is like learning another language. It takes a lot of patience, study, application, method, passion and above all perseverance.

What I can suggest is to do as much practice as possible by starting to rewrite the hundreds of examples you find in this guide. Try to memorize them and when you write the code, say it to yourself, in your mind (open bracket, close round brackets and so on). In the beginning, this helped me a lot to memorize better the various steps needed to write a program even if simple.

It is important not to feel like heroes when a program works but above all you should not be depressed when you cannot find a solution to your programming problems. The network is full of sites and blogs where you can always find a solution.

I hope that this guide has been useful for you in learning Python.

PYTHON FOR DATA ANALYSIS

A PRACTICAL GUIDE YOU CAN'T
MISS TO MASTER DATA USING
PYTHON. KEY TOOLS FOR DATA
SCIENCE, INTRODUCING YOU INTO
DATA MANIPULATION, DATA
VISUALIZATION, MACHINE
LEARNING.

ERICK THOMPSON

INTRODUCTION

D ata analysis plays an important part in many aspects of life today. A lot of important decisions are made based on data analytics. Companies need data to help them meet many of their goals. As the population of the world keeps growing, its customer base keeps expanding. In light of this, they must find ways of keeping their customers happy while at the same time meeting their business goals.

Given the nature of competition in the business world, it is not easy to keep customers happy. Competitors keep preying on each other's customers, and those who win have another challenge ahead - how to maintain the customers lest they slide back to their former business partners. This is one area where Data Analysis comes in handy.

To understand their customers better, companies rely on data. They collect all manner of data at each point of interaction with their customers. Data are useful in several ways. The companies learn more about their customers, thereafter clustering them according to their specific needs. Through such segmentation, the company can attend to the customers' needs better and hope to keep them satisfied for longer.

But, data analytics is not just about customers and the profit motive. It is also about governance. Governments are the biggest data consumers all over the world. They collect data about citizens, businesses, and every other entity that they interact with at any given point. This is important information because it helps in a lot of instances.

For planning purposes, governments need accurate data on their population so that funds can be allocated accordingly. Equitable distribution of resources is something that cannot be achieved without proper Data Analysis. Other than planning, there is also the security angle. To protect the country, the government must maintain different databases for different reasons. There are high profile individuals who must be accorded special security detail, top threats who must be monitored at all times, and so forth. To meet the security objective, the government has to obtain and maintain updated data on persons of interest at all times.

There is so much more to Data Analysis than corporate and government decisions. As a programmer, you are venturing into an industry that is challenging and exciting at the same time. Data doesn't lie unless it is manipulated, in which case you need insane Data Analysis and handling skills. As a data analyst, you will come across many challenges and problems that need solutions that can only be handled through Data Analysis. The way you interact with data can make a big difference, bigger than you can imagine.

There are several equipments you can use for Data Analysis. Many people use Microsoft Excel for Data Analysis and it works well for them. However, there are limitations of using Excel which you can overcome through Python. Learning Python is a good initiative, given that it is one of the easiest programming languages. It is a high-level programming language because its syntax is so close to the normal language we use.

For expert programmers, you have gone beyond learning about the basics of Python and graduated into using Python to solve real-world problems. Many problems can be solved through Data Analysis. The first challenge is usually understanding the issue at hand, then working on a data solution for it.

Knowledge of Python libraries is indeed important. It is by understanding these libraries that you can go on to become an expert data analyst with Python.

As you interact with data, you do understand the importance of cleaning data to ensure the outcome of your analysis is not flawed. You will learn how to go about this and build on that to make sure your work is perfect. Another challenge that many organizations have is protecting the integrity of data. You should try and protect your organization from using contaminated data. There are procedures you can make use of to make sure that you use clean data all the time.

Data is produced and stored in large amounts daily from automated systems. Learning Data Analysis through Python should help you process and extract information from data and make meaningful conclusions from them. One area where these skills will come in handy is forecasting. Through Data Analysis, you can create predictive models that should help your organization meet its objectives.

A good predictive model is only near as good as the quality of data introduced into it, the data modeling methods, and more importantly, the dataset used for the analysis. Beyond data handling and processing, one other important aspect of Data Analysis is visualization.

Visualization is about presentation. Your data model should be good enough for an audience to read and understand it at the first point of contact. Apart from the audience, you should also learn how to plot data on different visualizations to help you get an irregular idea of the nature of the data you are working with.

When you are done with Data Analysis, you should have a data model complete with visual concepts that will help in predicting outcomes and responses before you can proceed to the testing phase. Data analysis is a study that is currently in high demand in different fields. Knowing what to do, as well as when and how to handle data, is an important skill that you should not take lightly. Through this, you can build and test a hypothesis and go on to understand systems better.

CHAPTER - 1
INTRODUCTION TO PYTHON AND
DATA ANALYSIS

Data Science and Data Analysis

The words of data science and data analytics are often used interchangeably. However, these terms are completely different and have different implications for different businesses. Data science encompasses a variety of scientific models and methods that can be used to manipulate and survey structured, semi structured, and unstructured data. Tools and processes that can be used to make sense of gather insight from highly complex, unorganized and raw data set falls under the category of data science. Unlike data analytics that is targeted to verify a hypothesis, data science boils down to connecting data points to identify new patterns and insights that can be made use of in future planning for the business. Data science moves the business from inquiry to insights by providing a new perspective into their structured and unstructured data by identifying patterns that can allow businesses to increase efficiencies, reduce costs and recognize the new market opportunities.

Data science acts as a multidisciplinary blend of technology, machine learning algorithm development, statistical analysis, and data inference that provides businesses with enhanced capability to solve their most complex business problems. Data analytics falls under the category of data science and pertains more to reviewing and analyzing historical data to put it in context. Unlike data science, data analytics is characterized by low usage of artificial intelligence, predictive modeling and machine learning algorithms to gather insights from processed and structured data using standard SQL query commands. The seemingly nuanced differences between data analytics and data science can actually have a substantial impact on an organization.

Python as top languages for developers at top companies

When startups are planning a process of product development, they need to keep in mind and take note of different factors when it comes to choosing the right language for programming. Moreover, since many startups start from scratch, the budget available is often low, and this is why they very carefully consider factors like how swift the development would be, how popular and widely use the language is factors like the cost of libraries, integrations, and developers. In addition, the cost of security and scalability and not to forget stability. Due to these reasons, it is always preferred by startups around the world and especially in Silicon Valley to opt for a robust and strong technology like Python, which is established and deep-rooted.

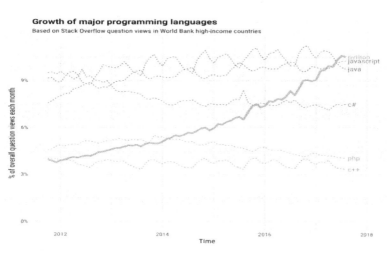

Growth of major programming languages
Based on Stack Overflow question views in World Bank high-income countries

This is not the start of technology. It has been around for more than as long as 30 years in the market, and it is so robust and established that it is still one of the tops and best languages for programming that ever existed. This means that Python is so established and widely used that even the latest innovations in the IT sector could not elbow it aside. According to a survey by BuiltWith, as many as one million websites out there are Python costumers and have been performing pretty amazingly with great returns. Credit goes to the robust programing language. Another survey about the popularity of Python by TIOBE INDEX reveals that an index called programming community index PCI that measures how popular the programing languages are has ranked Python as the third most famous and popular programing language around the world.

Python for Data Analysis

Python is among the most popular computer language programming tool initially created and designed by Guido Van Rossum in the late 1980s. Since its introduction into the computing world, Python has undergone multiple modifications and improvements, therefore, becoming among leading programming languages used by developers. The tool is dynamically typed, object-oriented, multi-paradigm, and imperative. It is used across different operating systems including Windows, Linux, Android, macOS, and iOS devices. Besides, it is compatible with both bit 32 and bit 64 gadgets of phones, laptops, and desktops.

Despite comprising of several areas essential for programmers, Python is easy to learn, especially when it comes to beginners with minimal knowledge in computer programming. Unlike most programming languages, Python accompanies an easy to use syntaxes where first time users can readily practice and become a pro within a few weeks. However, the programming processes may vary depending on the motive of the learner in programming. Despite accompanying multiple vocabularies and sometimes sophisticated tutorials for learning different programming techniques, engaging with Python is worth it to develop excellent programs.

CHAPTER - 2

PYTHON BASICS

N ow that we have look at Python and some of the benefits that come with it to ensure we get the full reasons why someone would want to use it for data analysis, it is time for us to go through some of the basics of writing code in Python. There are a lot of different parts that are all going to come together to help us make sure that we are writing our codes out well, and that we actually learn what Python is all about.

Python history

Python programming began at the fingertips of a Dutch programmer, name of Guido Van Rossum. He wrote the program sometime in the latter period of the '80s as a hobby project. Since its release to the public, Python has grown and evolved over time to be one of the most acclaimed, polished, and consistent languages in the world of computer programming.

According to Van Rossum, the conception of Python can be traced to a Christmas weekend in December 1989. He had begun working on his hobby project in his free time to develop an interpreter language—a successor to the ABC programming language to which Van Rossum helped develop. However, when the entire process of development came to an end, Python emerged as nothing short of a complete programming language in itself. Given its somewhat already weird history, the name "Python" draws even more questions to the identity of the programming language. Van Rossum had the Unix and C hackers as the target audience of his program, but more importantly, he was especially keen on the then famous TV sitcom—The Monty Python's Flying Circus. Van Rossum explained that he found the name "Python" not only suitable to his taste but appealing to his target audience, so he ran with it.

Installing Python

To install Python, visit https://www.python.org/. Navigate to the Downloads field where you'll proceed to download the latest Python version depending on your Operating system.

Python Comments

The next thing that we need to take a look at in the comments. These are going to be unique parts of any code that allow you to add in a little bit of a note or information into the code without it actually affecting the code or causing it to have an error.

If you would like to name a certain part of the code, or you want to leave a little message for yourself, or for another programmer who would take a look through your information and your code. You can explain what is going through that part of the code for yourself or someone else, get it a different name, or something else.

Working on the comments is going to be simple to work with. Each code is going to work with these comments in a slightly different manner, but in the Python language, we just need to use the # symbol ahead of the comment. You can have the comment be as long or short as you would like, and you can have as many of these in your code as you would like as well. The rule is to just keep this to a minimum as much as possible, though, to ensure the code stays nice and clean along the way.

Numbers

Numbers are a type of data type used to store numeric values only. Python supports three types of numbers. They include floats, integers, and complex numbers.

Unlike some programming languages where you declare the variable data type before using it, Python requires you to only declare the name of the variable, and then the equal sign and the assigned value.

```
age = 22
```

Floats

We use floats, also called real-numbers, to represent decimal numbers, and we frequently represent them with a decimal point. In Python, we can also represent floats in scientific notation using the exponential symbol. Example: 0.84e5 = 84000.0

Integers

In Python, we use Integers to represent 'whole' numerical values that do not have decimal points. Integers can be either positive or negative representation.

```
x = 10
y = -34
type(x)
type(y)
```

```
int
```

Complex Numbers

In python, we represent Complex numbers as x + yi where x and y represent float numbers, and i equals the square root of -1 (imaginary number). Complex numbers are not very common in Python programming but the language does support them.

Long

Long, also called long integers, are integers of unlimited size. We write them as integers followed by uppercase or lowercase L. Only Python2 supports this type of numbers.

To find the type of a variable, use the type() method built into python

Lists

Another topic that is going to show up when we work with Python is the differences between a list and a dictionary, and even a tuple. First, we are going to explore what the lists are like. The list is going to actually have the most versatility when it comes to types of objects that are used in Python. Some of the things that we will notice when working on these lists include

1. A list is going to be an ordered and mutable sequence of items. Because of this, it is something that we are able to slice, index, and change along the way. Each element is something that we are able to access using the position it has on the list. Python lists are going to work for most of the collection data structures, and since they are found as built-in, you do not have to go through the process of manually creating them.

2. Lists are going to be used for any object type, from strings to numbers and to more lists as well.

3. They are going to be accessed just like a string, which means that they are simple to use, and they will be variable in length. We are able to see them shrink and grow automatically as we use them.

4. List variables are going to be declared when we work with the brackets, and then the name of the variable will be ahead of it.

Tuples

Another option to explore is known as a tuple. Tuples are going to be used in Python to help hold together more than one object. Think of this as something that is similar to the list, but it is not going to have the extensive functionality that the list class is going to provide to us. One of the major features that we will like about these tuples is that they are going to be immutable, similar to strings, which means we are not able to modify them.

Even though modification is not allowed here, you are able to take portions of some of the existing tuples and use it to make a new tuple. Lists are going to be declared with a square bracket, and then we are able to change them as needed. However, the tuple is going to be found in the parentheses, and we are not able to change them at all.

Dictionaries

A dictionary is much like an address book. If you know the name of the person you wish to contact, you can obtain the details of that person. The name of the person is the key, while the details of the person are the value.

The key that you use in a dictionary should be an immutable data type; that is, it can be a number, tuple, or string. The value can be anything. A dictionary is a mutable data type, and it is for this reason that you can add, modify or remove any pairs from the dictionary. The keys are mapped to an object, and it is for this reason that a dictionary is also known as mappings. This will show you that a dictionary behaves differently to a sequence.

A dictionary can be used anywhere you want to store a value or attribute that will describe an entity or a concept. For instance, you can use a dictionary to count the number of instances of a specific state or object. Since every key has a unique identifier, you cannot have duplicate values for the same key. Therefore, the key can be used to store the items in the input data, and the values can store the result of the calculation.

Python Function

Now that we have a better idea of how the classes are going to work in Python and why these are so important to some of the work that we want to create in this language, it is time to move on to some of the other parts of coding that are important for our goals as well. In particular, we are going to spend a bit of time looking at the steps that we are able to follow in order to create a function in the Python language.

A function, to start with, is just going to be a block of code, any block of code, which is only going to run when the compiler calls it out. You are able to pass on data, which will be known as a parameter, over to your function to ensure that it is going to work in the manner that you want. And then, as the function continues to do its job, it is able to return data as a result as well.

With this in mind, we need to take a look at some of the steps that we are able to use in order to create and then call one of the functions that we want to work with. This is fairly simple because we are able to define one of these functions with the use of the def keyword. The code that you can use to create one of these functions includes:

def my_function():

print("Hello from a function")

The code that we will focus on here is going to have a function that just has one argument, which is known as (fname) when we are able to call up the function, we will pass along the first name, which is the going to be used inside of the function to help us get the full name printed off as well.

Now that we have brought up both the idea of a parameter and that of an argument, we need to figure out which one is going to be the best one to use for our codes. The terms of argument and parameter can be used for the same thing because both of them are going to include information that is passed on over to the function.

When we look at this from the perspective of the function, the parameter is going to be a variable that is listed inside of the parentheses in the definition of the function. The argument, on the other hand, is going to be the value that has been sent to the function when it is called out. We can use both in a similar manner along the way, though.

We can also work with the idea that is known as recursion. Python is also going to accept what is known as function recursion, which means that the defined function is able to come through and call itself.

Recursion is going to be a common concept in programming and mathematics. It means that a function is going to call itself. This has the benefit of allowing programming to loop through the data to reach the result that we are working with.

If you want to work with recursion, you need to be careful with the work that you handle here. It is easy to mess up and start writing a function that is never going to terminate, or one that is going to use too much memory or processing power to get the work done. However, when it is written

out in the correct manner, it is possible for recursion to be efficient, and an elegant approach, mathematically, when you do your programming.

Strings

Now it is time to take a look at something that is known as the Python strings. We did take a look at these a bit with some of the other topics, but now it is time to give them a look of their own. To make this process simple, remember that this string is going to just be a series of text characters that are found in your code and can help you to get things done.

There are a few different operators that we need to focus on when we want to handle our strings in Python. An operator is going to be a simple symbol that we are able to use to perform the operations that are necessary inside of our code. Some of the operators that we need to spend the most time looking through when we work with Python include:

- Concatenation operator: This is the operator that you would want to use when it is time to concatenate strings.

- Repetition operator: This is the operator that you will use in order to create many copies of a string. You can choose how many times you would like to repeat the string.

- Slice operator: This is the operator that is going to look through your string and then retrieve the specific character that you want from there. Any time that you use this one, you would need to remember that zero is going to be the first character of the string.

- Range slice operator: This is the operator that is going to retrieve a range of characters from your index, rather than just one character. If you just want to showcase one word or one part of your string, you would use this kind of operator.

- In operator: This operator is going to search for a specified character in a target string. If the character is present somewhere in the string, then you will get an answer of True returned to you. If that character is not inside the string, then you will get an answer of False returned to you.

- No in operator: This is the operator that will work in the opposite manner as the in operator. It is going to search for a specified character in your string. But if the operator is not able to find that character in the string, then you will get the True answer returned. If that character is found in the string, then it is going to return False.

Boolean

Python Boolean is a data type that contains only two number diagrams. Both values generally represent true or false, which is logical or boolean algebra. In most cases, the two qualities in Boolean algebra are generally consistent. Contingent upon how Boolean impacts or portrays a circumstance, restrictive proclamations are related to activities on how the designer chooses. In this, the value represented by logic does not necessarily have to be Boolean.

Loop

There are actually a few different types of loops that we are able to work with when it comes to Python. These are going to be nice because they take out some of the work. If there is a part of the code that you would like to see repeat itself a bunch of times, rather than rewriting out that part of code over and over again, we would simply turn it into a loop. In specific, we are going to take a look at what the loop is about and how we can utilize this for our needs too.

To start, the loop is going to be used to help us iterate over one of the sequences that we want to use. This could be a string, a set, a dictionary, a tuple, or a list. This is going to be less like the keyword that we see with other coding languages, and it is more like the iterator method for other OOP languages.

When we focus on the loop, we are going to spend some time executing a set of specific statements that we want to see taken care of. This is going to happen one time for each item on the list, tuple, or set. A good example that we can look at here is below:

```
fruits = ["apple", "banana", "cherry"]

for x in fruits:

print(x)
```

Now in some cases, we also have to make sure that we add in a break statement. This will ensure that the code will know where to stop and that it is not going to keep going in an endless loop that we are not able to stop. This will effectively freeze up our computers and make it hard to work with them without exiting the whole program. Set up the broken part in this to ensure that it will behave in the manner that you want.

CHAPTER - 3

ESSENTIAL PYTHON LIBRARIES AND INSTALLATION

What is Matplotlib?

There are a lot of different libraries that we are able to work with when it is time to handle visuals and other work of data analysis inside of our Python language. But the library that we are going to spend some time taking a look at is one that is meant to work with the idea of data visualization and why this is so important to some of the work that we want to accomplish.

To start with, you will find that matplotlib is going to be a plotting library that is set up to work with Python. It is also going to be a numerical mathematics extension that works off the arrays that we see in NumPy. This means that if we want to work with the matplotlib library, we need to first make sure that we have NumPy, and sometimes other libraries as well, on our system and ready to go as well.

When we are working with Matplotlib, you will find that it is useful when it is time to provide an API that is object-oriented for embedding plots into applications that will work with some of the toolkits for GUI that is general-purpose. There is also going to be a procedural interface based on a state machine that will work similar to MATLAB, although these are both going to be completely different things from one another, and it is important to work with them in a different manner.

The matplotlib is a great library to work with, and it was originally written by John D. Hunter. It is also going to impress a lot of new programmers because it has a development community that is active. It is also going to be distributed with a license that is BSD so that it is easier for us to use the way that we would like overall.

There are a lot of really cool options that you are able to work with when it is time to handle the matplotlib library, and this opens up a lot of opportunities for you when it is time to pick out the different choices in visuals. There are many of these that you are able to work with, and thanks to the way that matplotlib is set up, you will be able to pick out almost any kind of visual that you would like to work with as well.

This means that if you want to make a chart, a pie graph, a bar graph, a histogram, or some other kind of chart, this library is going to have a lot of the additional parts that we are looking for when it is time to handle your data. Make sure to take a look at some of the different options that are provided with this library, and then pay attention to what we are able to do with them before picking the one that is the best for you.

There are also going to be a number of different toolkits that you are able to handle when it is time to work with Matplotlib. These toolkits are important because they are going to help us to really extend out the amount of functionality that we will see with this library. Depending on the one that you would like to work with, some of them are going to be separate kinds of downloads, and some are going to ship along with the source code that is found in this library, but their dependencies are going to be found outside of this library, so we have to pay attention to this as well. Some of the different toolkits that we are able to work with include:

1. The basemap: This is going to be a map plotting tool that we are able to use to help out with different types of projects of a map, coastlines, and political boundaries that we are going to see in here.

2. Cartopy: This is another good one to work with when it is time to handle maps and some of that kind of work. This is going to be a mapping library that will have object-oriented map project definitions and arbitrary point lines, image transformation, and even polygon capabilities as well.

3. This one can also come with a number of Excel tools if you would like to work with these as well. This makes it easier for us to use Excel as our database, and you will easily be able to set this up so that you are able to exchange data from your matplotlib library and Excel.

4. GTK tools that are going to allow us the ability to interface and work with the GTK+ library if you would like.

5. The Qt interface.

6. The ability to work with 3-D plots to help out with some of the visuals that you are going to want to use along the way.

7. Natgrid: This is going to be an interface that will allow us into the library of natgrid for gridding irregularly spaced data when you would like.

There are a few other libraries that help with visuals if you would like, but we have to remember that this is one of the best ones to work with, and they will keep things as simple and easy to use as possible. And with all of the added and nice features that are going to come with this, you will be able to see some great results with your visuals as well.

Statsmodel

Statsmodel is another Python library for data science widely used for statistical analysis. Statsmodel is a Python library used to perform statistical tests and implement various statistical models for extensive data exploration. Statsmodel was developed at Stanford University by Professor Jonathan Taylor. Compared with Scikit-learn, statsmodel has algorithms for classical statistics and econometrics.

They include submodules such as:

- Regression models such as linear mixed-effects models, robust linear models, generalized linear models and linear regression.

- Nonparametric methods such as Kernel density estimation and kernel regression.

- Analysis of variance.

- Time series analysis

- Visualization of statistical model results

SciPy

What's SciPy for?

Python customers who prefer a quick and effective math library can use NumPy, however NumPy through itself isn't very task-focused.

How SciPy 1.0 helps with data science

SciPy has always been beneficial for supplying handy and extensively used equipment for working with math and statistics.

The set off for bringing the SciPy challenge to model 1.0, in accordance with core developer Ralf Gommers, used to be specifically a consolidation of how the mission once ran and managed. But it additionally covered a procedure for non-stop integration for the MacOS and Windows builds, as nicely as a suitable aid for prebuilt Windows binaries. This ultimate characteristic ability Windows customers can now use SciPy by not having to soar through extra hoops.

Where to obtain SciPy?

SciPy binaries can be gotten from the Python Package Index, or via typing pip installation scipy. Source code is reachable on GitHub.

Pandas

Pandas are going to be a big name when we want to use the Python language to analyze the data we have, and it is actually one of the most used tools that we can bring out when it comes to data wrangling and data munging. Pandas are open-sourced, similar to what we see with some of the other libraries and extensions that are found in Python world. It is also free to use and will be able to handle all of the different parts of your data analysis.

There is a lot that you will enjoy when working with the Pandas library, but one of the neat things is that this library is able to take data, of almost any format that you would like, and then create a Python object out of it. This is known as a data frame and will have the rows and columns that you need to keep it organized. It is going to look similar to what we are used to seeing with an Excel sheet.

To start with, we are going to use this library to help us to load and save our data. When you want to use this particular library to help out with data analysis, you will find that you can use it in three different manners. These include:

1. You can use it to convert a Python dictionary or list, or aa array in NumPy to a data frame with the help of this library.

2. You can use it to open up a local file with Pandas. This is usually going to be done in a CSV file, but it is also possible to do it in other options like a delimited text file or in Excel.

3. You can also open a remote file or a database like JSON or CSV on one of the websites through a URL, or you can use it to read out the information that is found on an SQL table or database.

Numpy

NumPy is the key bundle for logical registering in Python. It is a Python library that offers a multidimensional showcase object, unique inferred objects, (for example, veiled clusters and grids), and a grouping of schedules for rapid tasks on clusters, consisting of numerical, coherent, structure control, arranging, choosing, I/O, discrete Fourier changes, quintessential straight variable based math, indispensable factual activities, irregular reenactment and substantially more.

At the center of the NumPy bundle, is the ndarray object. This exemplifies n-dimensional varieties of homogeneous information types, with numerous activities being carried out in assembling code for execution. There are a few significant contrasts between NumPy well-known shows and the popular Python groupings:

- NumPy clusters have a constant measurement at creation, distinctive to Python documents (which can advance progressive). Changing the measurement of a ndarray will make some other exhibit and erase the first.

- The aspects in a NumPy cluster are altogether required to be of comparable data type, and in consequence will be a comparative dimension in memory. The unique case: one can have the sorts of (Python, inclusive of NumPy) objects, alongside these strains taking into account sorts of quite a number estimated components.

- NumPy reveals encourage stepped forward numerical and one of a kind kinds of things to do on massive portions of information. Ordinarily, such duties are carried out more productively and with much less code than is conceivable utilizing Python's worked in successions.

- Creating lots of logical and scientific Python-based bundles are making use of NumPy exhibits; however these in most cases bolsters Python-succession input, they convert such contribution to NumPy clusters earlier than preparing, and they frequently yield NumPy clusters. At the end of the day, so as to efficaciously utilize a great deal (maybe even most) of the present logical/scientific Python-based programming, truly realizing how to make use of Python's labored in succession kinds is missing - one likewise has to realize how to utilize NumPy exhibits.

The focus on grouping size and velocity is particularly widespread in logical registering. As a fundamental model, consider the instance of growing each and every aspect in a 1-D grouping with the referring to issue in another succession of a comparable length. In the match that the statistics are put away in two Python records, an and b, we should emphasize each component:

This creates the proper answer, but on the off chance that an and b each comprise a massive number of numbers, we will pay the price for the wasteful elements of circling in Python. We ought to reap a comparable assignment substantially extra swiftly in C by means of composing (for

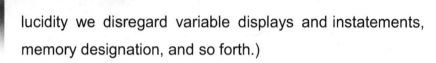

lucidity we disregard variable displays and instatements, memory designation, and so forth.)

This spares all the overhead engaged with interpreting the Python code and controlling Python objects, yet to the detriment of the advantages picked up from coding in Python. Moreover, the coding work required increments with the dimensionality of our information. On account of a 2-D cluster, for instance, the C code (abbreviated as in the past) grows to NumPy offers us the quality of the two universes: thing by-component things to do are the "default mode" when an ndarray is included, but the aspect by-component undertaking is swiftly carried out with the aid of pre-gathered C code. In NumPy

$c = a * b$

Does what the preceding fashions do, at shut C speeds, but with the code effortlessness we count on from something dependent on Python. Surely, the NumPy phrase is lots less complex! This last mannequin represents two of NumPy's highlights which are the premise of a lot of its capacity: vectorization and broadcasting.

Vectorization depicts the non appearance of any unequivocal circling, ordering, and so forth., in the code - these matters are occurring, obviously, honestly "in the background" in advanced, pre-incorporated C code. Vectorized code has numerous preferences, among which are:

- vectorized code is steadily brief and less difficult to peruse
- fewer lines of code for the most section implies fewer bugs
- the code all the extra closely takes after well-known numerical documentation (making it simpler, commonly, to precise code scientific develops)
- vectorization brings about greater "Pythonic" code. Without vectorization, our code would be covered with wasteful and tough to peruse for circles.

Broadcasting is the term used to depict the sore issue by-component behavior of activities; for the most section talking, in NumPy all tasks, wide variety juggling tasks, yet coherent, piece shrewd, utilitarian, and so forth., elevate on in this verifiable factor by-component design, i.e., they communicate. Besides, in the model over, an and bought to be multidimensional types of a comparable shape, or a scalar and an exhibit, or even two sorts of with a variety of shapes, gave that the little cluster is "expandable" to the kingdom of the higher so that the subsequent talk is unambiguous. For factor by way of point "rules" of broadcasting see numpy.doc.broadcasting.

Scikit-Learn

You are not going to get too far when it comes to working on a data analysis if you do not bring in the Scikit-Learn library. This is going to be seen as one of the simple and efficient tools that you can use for data mining and for completing data analysis. What is so great about this one is that it is going to be accessible to anyone, and it can be reusable in many contexts as well. It is also going to come to us with a commercially usable license and it is open source, so we are able to work with it and use it in the manner that we want. Some of the features that we are likely to see with this one include:

1. It can help with problems of classification. This is where it helps us to identify which category a particular object is going to belong with.

2. It can help with some problems of regression. This is where it is able to predict a continuous value attribute associated with the object.

3. It can help with some problems with clustering. This is where we are going to have an automatic grouping of objects that are similar in the sets.

4. It can help us complete something that is known as dimensionality reduction. This is where we are able to reduce the number of random variables that we want to normalize in all of this.

IPython

Another environment that we can look at is the IPython environment. This is a bit different from some of the others, but it is going to help us to get some more work done. IPython is going to be a shell that is interactive and works well with the Python programming language. It is there to help us to work with many good source codes and can do some tab completion, work with some additional shell syntax, and enhanced introspection all on one.

This is going to be one of the alternatives that we can get with the Python interpreter. A shell is more interactive that can be used for some of the computing that you want to do in Python. In addition, it can provide us with more features based on what we would like to do with our work.

You can enjoy several features when working on the IPython environment. First, it will help you to run more shell commands that are native. When you run any of the interpreters that you would like to use, the interpreter should have a number of commands that are built-in. These commands are sometimes going to collide with the native commands of the shell.

For example, if we wanted to work with the traditional interpreter of Python and we typed in the code of "cd" after the interpreter loaded up, you would get an error on your screen. The reason for this error is that the interpreter is not going to recognize this command. This is a command that is native to the terminal of your computer, but not to the Python interpreter. On the other hand, IPython is going to have some more support for those native shell commands so you can utilize them in your work.

IPython is also a good one to work with when it comes to syntax highlighting. One of the first things that we are going to notice about this is that it provides us with syntax highlighting. This means that it is going to use color to help us look over the different parts of the Python code. If you type in x = 10 to your terminal, you would be able to see how the IPython environment is going to highlight this code in a variety of colors. The syntax highlighting is going to be a big improvement over what we see in the default interpreter of Python and can help us to read the code a bit better.

Another benefit of working with IPython is that it works with the proper indentation to help you out. If you have done some coding in the past, you know that it does pay attention to the indentation and whitespace. IPython recognizes this and then automatically provides you with the right indentation as you type the code into this interpreter. This makes things a lot easier as you go through the process.

This environment is also going to work with tab completion. IPython is going to provide us with some tab-completion so that we do not have to worry about handling this. This helps to ensure that the compiler is going to know what is going on with the codes that we write and that all of the work will show up in the manner that you want.

Documentation is another feature that we are able to see with IPython, and it is going to help us to work well with the code. Doing the autocompletion of tabs is going to be useful because it will provide us with a list of all the methods that are possible inside of the specific module. With all of the options at your disposal, you may be confused at what one particular method does. In addition, this is where the documentation of IPython can come into play. It will provide you with the documentation for any method you work with to save time and hassle.

Then the final benefit that we are going to look at here is that IPython can help with pasting blocks of code. IPython is going to be excellent when we want to paste large amounts of Python code. You can grab any block of the Python code, paste it into this environment, and you should get the result of a code that is properly indented and ready to go on this environment. It is as easy as all that.

You can choose to work with the regular Python environment if you would like, but there are also many benefits to upgrading and working with this one as well, especially when you are working with something like data science and completing your own data analysis.

CHAPTER - 4

IPYTHON AND JUPITER

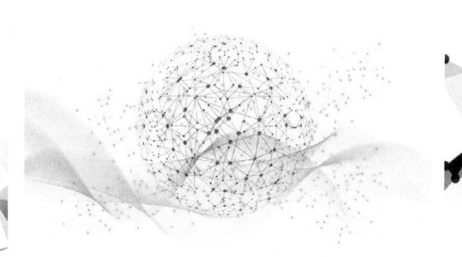

IPython

IPython same as Interactive Python is a capable toolkit that allows you to experience Python interactively. It has two main components: a dependent Python Shell interface, and Jupyter kernels.

These components have many features, such as:

Persistent input history

- Caching of outputs

- Code completition

- Support for 'magic' commands

- Highly customizable settings

- Syntax highlighting

- Session logging

- Access to system Shell

- Support for python's debugger and profiler

Now, let's go into each of these components and see how these features come to life.

IPython Shell

The objective of this Shell is to provide a superior experience than the default Python REPL.

To run the IPython Shell you just need to call the command bellow on your system console.

§ Interface

At first glance, the IPython Shell looks like a normal boring Shell, some initial version information and some user tips. However, it has great features that make it shine.

§ Help

You can type "?" after an accessible object at any time you want more details about it.

§ Code Completition

You can press "TAB" key at any time to trigger the code completition.

§ Syntax Highlight

The code is automatically highlighted depending on the variables and keywords you are using.

§ Run External Commands

External commands can be run directly using "!" at the beginning of the input.

§ Magic Commands

Magic commands add incredible capabilities to IPython. Some commands are shown bellow:

%time – Shows the time to execute the command.

%timeit – Shows the mean and standard deviation of the time to execute the command.

%pdb – Run the code in debug mode, creating breakpoints on uncaught exceptions.

%matplotlib – This command arranges all the setup needed to IPython work correctly with matplotlib, this way

IPython can display plots that are outputs of running code in new windows.

There are multiple magic commands that be used on IPython Shell, for a full list of the built-in commands check this link or type "%lsmagic".

Jupiter Notebook

Getting started with Jupyter Notebook (IPython)

The Jupyter Note pad is an open-source web application that permits you to produce and share files that contain live code, formulas, visualizations and narrative text. Utilizes consist of information cleansing and change, mathematical simulation, analytical modeling, information visualization, artificial intelligence, and far more.

Jupyter has assistance for over 40 various shows languages and Python is among them. Python is a requirement (Python 3.3 or higher, or Python 2.7) for setting up the Jupyter Notebook itself.

Setting up Jupyter utilizing Anaconda

Set up Python and Jupyter utilizing the Anaconda Distribution, which includes Python, the Jupyter Notebook, and other typically utilized bundles for clinical computing and information science. You can download Anaconda's newest Python3 variation.

Command to run the Jupyter notebook:

When the Notepad opens in your Internet browser, you will see the Notebook Dashboard, which will reveal a list of the notepads, files, and subdirectories in the directory site where the Notepad server was started. Most of the time, you will want to begin a Notepad server in the greatest level directory site consisting of notepads. Typically, this will be your house directory site.

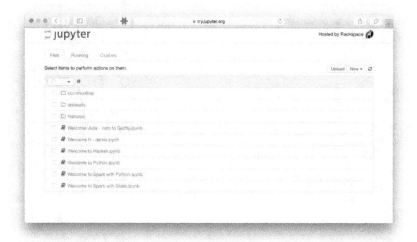

CHAPTER - 5

NUMPY FOR NUMERICAL DATA PROCESSING

Object ndarray

An ndarray object is an n-dimensional structure that stores data. Only one type of data is stored in a ndarray. We can have ndarray objects with as many dimensions as necessary (a dimension for a vector, two dimensions for a matrix ...).

Ndarray objects are a "minimal" format for storing data. Ndarray objects have specific optimized methods that allow you to do calculations extremely fast. It is possible to store ndarray in files to reduce the necessary resources. The ndarray has two important attributes: the type and the shape. When creating a ndarray, we can define the type and the shape or let Python infer these values.

To use NumPy, we always use the same method: import numpy as np. From now on, we use the term array to designate a ndarray object.

Building An Array

The easiest way to build an array is to use the function of

```
NumPy: np.array ()
```

We can create an array from a list with:

```
array_de_liste np.array = ([1,4,7,9])
```

This function takes other parameters including the type, that is to say, the typical elements of the array. The types are very varied in NumPy. Outside of classical types such as int, float, boolean or str, there are many types in NumPy. We will come back to this in the next paragraph.

We can create an array from a series of numbers with the function range () which works like the Python range () function.

```
In []: array_range = np.arange (10)

print (array_range)

[0123456789]
```

Apart from the arrange () function of NumPy, we can use the linspace () function which will return numbers in an interval with a constant distance from one to the other:

```
In  []:  array_linspace  =  np.linspace  (0,9,10)  print
(array_linspace)
```

We see that 0 is the lower bound, 9 is the upper bound and we divide into 10 values. We can specify each time the dtype = in each function. From specific formats, there are functions to generate arrays.

Creating and modify Arrays

The development of Python-related data has mostly been done thanks to a package absolutely central for Python. This is NumPy (an abbreviation of Numerical Python). NumPy makes it possible to transform a very classical programming language in a numerical oriented language. It has been developed and improved for many years and now offers an extremely well-organized system of data management.

The central element of NumPy is the array that stores values in a structure supporting all types of advanced calculations. The strength of NumPy lies largely in the fact that it is not coded directly in Python but in C, which gives it an unequaled processing speed with the "classic" Python code. The goal of the NumPy developers is to provide a simple, fast and comprehensive tool to support the various developments in the field of digital processing. NumPy is often presented at the same time as SciPy, a package for scientific computing based on structure from NumPy.

NumPy is useful for both novice and seasoned developers seasoned. ndarray, which are n-dimensional structures, are used by all Python users to process the data. Moreover, the tools allowing to interface Python with other languages such as C or Fortran are not used only by more advanced developers.

Broadcasting

The notion of broadcasting is linked to the fact of managing vector computations on arrays of various sizes. NumPy allows you to do calculations on arrays with different sizes. The simplest rule is:

Two dimensions are compatible when they are equal or if one of the two is of dimension 1. Broadcasting is a way of extending large arrays to adapt them to operations on operators with larger dimensions.

Examples of broadcasting:

If you have two arrays built as follows:

```
In []: arr1 = np.array ([1,4,7,9])

arr2 = np.ones (3)

arr1 + arr2

shapes (4,) (3,)

In []: arr3 = np.ones ((3,4))

arr1 + OFF3

Out []: array ([[2,5,8,10],

[2,5,8,10]

[2,5,8,10]])
```

In the first case, the two arrays have a first dimension that does not have the same size, we get an error. In the second case, we see that the two arrays have a common dimension (4). Therefore, the addition of the arr1 values is done for each value of the arr3 array. If, for example, we want to apply a transformation to an image that has been preferably transformed into the array, the dimensions of the images will be: (1000, 2000, 3). You can refer to the following paragraph for details on the characteristics of an image. Let's apply a transformation vector of dimension 3, and we will have:

```
In []: image.shape

Out []: (1000, 2000, 3)

In []: transf = np.array ([100, 255, 34])

transf.shape

Out []: (3,)

In []: new_image = image / transf

new_image.shape

Out []: (1000, 2000, 3)
```

The vector transf is applied to all the pixels, even if the dimensions do not correspond to lay only partially. We divide the first color by 100, the second by 255 and the third by 34. We will come back later to the treatment of images with NumPy.

Structured Arrays

The arrays we have used so far are arrays had only one type and no index other than the numerical index. Structural arrays are arrays in which several types can cohabit with names associated with these "columns". These arrays are not used much in practice but it is important to know their existence. We can create this type of arrays using:

```
In []: array_struct = np.array ([[('Client A', 900, 'Paris'),

('Client B', 1200, 'Lyon')],

dtype = [('Clients', 'U10'),

('CA', 'int'), ('City', 'U10')])

In []: array_struct

Out []: array ([[('Client A', 900, 'Paris'), ('Client B', 1200, 'Lyon')],

dtype = [('Clients', '<U10'), ('CA', '<i4'), ('City', '<U10')])
```

We see here that the array is created as a series of tuples with the values of a line. Here we have three columns in our array and two lines. The part of type is very important because it allows defining the name and the type of a column.

We use as types <U10 which is a type of NumPy for character strings of less than 10 characters. To get a column in our array, just do:

```
In []: array_struct ['Clients']
```

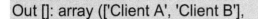

```
Out []: array (['Client A', 'Client B'],

dtype = '<U10')
```

To extract a value, we can use:

```
In []: array_struct ['CA'] [0]

Out []: 900
```

Nevertheless, this approach is not our preference. When we have data of different types with non-numerical indexes, we are interested in DataFrames and Pandas Series rather than structured arrays.

Operations and Functions

Numpy arrays, support arithmetic operations as expected. Here we will see some caveats of Broadcasting and built-in functions of the arrays.

Basic Operations

Same basic operations present in standard Python are also present in Numpy arrays. In this case, the operation between arrays of same shape results in another array.

Advanced Operations

There is also support for operations and transformations beyond the basics. Some advanced matrix operations are easily usable by functions in the linalg name space, attributes and methods of the object. For example, matrix product, determinant, inverse, etc.

CHAPTER - 6

PANDAS AND DATA MANIPULATION

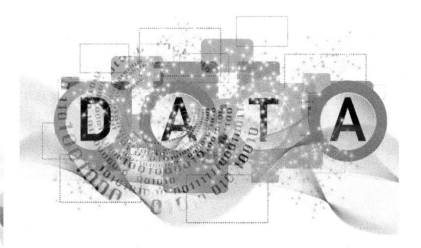

Pandas Installation

For installing Python Pandas, you need to go to the command line or terminal and then type "pip install pandas". Otherwise, in case you have anaconda installed on your computer, you may type in "conda install pandas". When this installation is finished go to the IDE, which may be PyCharm or Jupyter, and just import it with the command, "import pandas as pd." By moving forward for

Python Pandas topic let us take a closer look at some of the operations it performs.

Basic Structures in Pandas

With some of this in mind, it is time for us to go through a few of the different things that we are able to do with the Pandas code. First, we need to look at the data structures. There are two of these data structures that we are able to work with, including the series and the DataFrame.

The first one here is the series. This is going to be similar to what we are able to work with when it comes to a one-dimensional array. It is able to go through and store data of any type. The values of a Pandas Series are going to be mutable, but you will find that the size of our series is going to be immutable, and we are not able to change them later.

The first element in this series is going to be given an index of 0. Then the last element that is going to be found in this kind of index is N-1 because N is going to be the total number of elements that we put into our series. To create one of our own Series in Pandas, we need to first go through the process of importing the package of Pandas through the insert command of Python. The code that we are able to use, including:

Import pandas as pd

Then we can go through and create one of our own Series. We are going to invoke the method of pd.Series() and then pass on the array. This is simple to work with. The code that we are able to use to help us work with this includes:

Series1 = pd.Series([1, 2, 3, 4])

We need to then work with the print statement in order to display the contents of the Series. You can see that when you run this one, you have two columns. The first one is going to be the first one with numbers starting from the index of 0 like we talked about before, and then the second one is going to be the different elements that we added to our series. The first column is going to denote the indexes for the elements.

However, you could end up with an error if you are working with the display Series. The major cause of this error is that the Pandas library is going to take some time to look for the amount of information that is displayed, this means that you need to provide the sys output information. You are also able to go through this with the help of a NumPy array like we talked about earlier. This is why we need to make sure that when we are working with the Pandas library, we also go through and install and use the NumPy library as well.

The second type of data structure that we are able to work with here will include the DataFrames. These are going to often come in as a table. It is going to be able to organize the data into columns and rows, which is going to turn it into a two-dimensional data structure. This means that we have the potential to have columns that are of a different type, and the size of the DataFrame that we want to work with will be mutable, and then it can be modified.

To help us to work with this and create one of our own, we need to either go through and start out a new one from scratch, or we are going to convert other data structures, like the arrays for NumPy into the DataFrame.

Pandas DataFrame

A Pandas DataFrame is probably the most used data structure offered by Pandas. A Pandas DataFrame is a rectangular table that contains an ordered collection of columns. A DataFrame column can each consist of different data types such as Booleans, strings, integers, etc. Unlike a series, a Pandas DataFrame has both rows and column indices. The best way to think of a Pandas as a DataFrame is like a spreadsheet document, or, on a more technical side, a dictionary of Pandas series sharing a unique index.

The most common way to create a Pandas DataFrame is by passing a python dictionary that contains equal length lists or a Numpy array to the DataFrame function.

```
In [7]:  index = ['Barack Obama','Abraham Lincoln','John F Kennedy','George Washington','Franklin Roosevelt']
         data = {"Years":[8,4,2,8,12], "Number":[44,16,35,1,32]}

In [8]:  dataFrame = pd.DataFrame(data, index=index)

In [9]:  dataFrame

Out[9]:
```

	Years	Number
Barack Obama	8	44
Abraham Lincoln	4	16
John F Kennedy	2	35
George Washington	8	1
Franklin Roosevelt	12	32

First, we create a list containing the most popular presidents in the USA. Next, we create a dictionary containing their service years and the number which they served as president. Finally, we pass the data to the DataFrame function and their names as the index for the data. That results in a data frame containing the names of the presidents as the index, their service years and column 1 and their service number as column 2.

NOTE: Use Jupyter notebook while working with DataFrames as the formatting is friendly —HTML.

To retrieve a column in a Pandas DataFrame, we use either the dictionary notation —where we use the column name by using the attribute.

```
In [22]:  dataFrame['Presidents']

Out[22]:  0          Barack Obama
          1       Abraham Lincoln
          2        John F Kennedy
          3     George Washington
          4    Franklin Roosevelt
          Name: Presidents, dtype: object
```

```
In [24]:  dataFrame.Presidents

Out[24]:  0          Barack Obama
          1       Abraham Lincoln
          2        John F Kennedy
          3     George Washington
          4    Franklin Roosevelt
          Name: Presidents, dtype: object
```

Note that retrieving a column from a Pandas DataFrame produces a Pandas Series with its unique indices. This shows that a Pandas DataFrame consists of many Pandas Series. If you call the type function off the column, you will get a Pandas.core.series.Series data type.

```
In [25]:  type(dataFrame.Presidents)

Out[25]:  pandas.core.series.Series
```

We can also retrieve the rows of a Pandas DataFrame using a special loc attribute.

```
In [16]:  dataFrame.loc['Abraham Lincoln']

Out[16]:  Years     4
          Number    16
          Name: Abraham Lincoln, dtype: int64
```

NOTE: Depending on the method you use to execute the code used in the book, you might need to use the row number instead of the president's name and vice versa.

You can modify the Pandas dataframe columns by creating new ones and adding values to them. Let us add state column in our President's DataFrame as shown:

```
In [18]: dataFrame['State'] = ['Hawaii','Kentucky','Massachusetts','Virginia','New
```

```
In [19]: dataFrame
Out[19]:
```

	Years	Number	Country	State
Barack Obama	8	44	USA	Hawaii
Abraham Lincoln	4	16	USA	Kentucky
John F Kennedy	2	35	USA	Massachusetts
George Washington	8	1	USA	Virginia
Franklin Roosevelt	12	32	USA	New York

We pass the columns we want to add as a list followed by their corresponding values in respective order. Ensure to match the length of the DataFrame while assigning lists or arrays to a column to prevent occasions of missing data.

It is also important to note that assigning values to columns that do not exist will automatically create the column and assign to it the specified value.

To delete a column within a Pandas DataFrame, we use the del keyword, which is similar to how we delete a python dictionary. To illustrate column deletion, let us add a column called California and fill it with Boolean values – true if a president is from California and False if not.

```
In [21]: dataFrame['california'] = dataFrame.State == 'California'
```

```
In [22]: dataFrame
```
Out[22]:

	Years	Number	Country	State	california
Barack Obama	8	44	USA	Hawaii	False
Abraham Lincoln	4	16	USA	Kentucky	False
John F Kennedy	2	35	USA	Massachusetts	False
George Washington	8	1	USA	Virginia	False
Franklin Roosevelt	12	32	USA	New York	False

Using the del keyword, we can remove this column as shown below:

```
In [23]: del dataFrame['california']
```

```
In [24]: dataFrame
```
Out[24]:

	Years	Number	Country	State
Barack Obama	8	44	USA	Hawaii
Abraham Lincoln	4	16	USA	Kentucky
John F Kennedy	2	35	USA	Massachusetts
George Washington	8	1	USA	Virginia
Franklin Roosevelt	12	32	USA	New York

Now if we look at the existing columns within the DataFrame, we get four main columns as:

```
In [25]: dataFrame.columns
Out[25]: Index(['Years', 'Number', 'Country', 'State'], dtype='object')
```

Upon performing the del operation on the DataFrame, the returned column contains an actual view of the underlying data, which means that the operation occurs in-place, and any modifications undertaken on a section of the Pandas series also broadcasts to the original DataFrame.

You can copy a part of the Pandas array using the copy method. If a DataFrame does not have index and column name set, you can use the name attribute to accomplish this as shown below:

```
In [37]: dataFrame.index.name = ''; dataFrame.columns.name='Name'

In [38]: dataFrame
Out[38]:
```

Name	Years	Number	Country	State
Barack Obama	8	44	USA	Hawaii
Abraham Lincoln	4	16	USA	Kentucky
John F Kennedy	2	35	USA	Massachusetts
George Washington	8	1	USA	Virginia
Franklin Roosevelt	12	32	USA	New York

To get the values contained in a DataFrame, you can use the values attribute which returns a two-dimensional Numpy ndarrays, which is similar to the Pandas Series.

```
In [40]: dataFrame.values
Out[40]: array([[8, 44, 'USA', 'Hawaii'],
               [4, 16, 'USA', 'Kentucky'],
               [2, 35, 'USA', 'Massachusetts'],
               [8, 1, 'USA', 'Virginia'],
               [12, 32, 'USA', 'New York']], dtype=object)
```

In a scenario where the DataFrame's columns are of different data types, the data type of the values array is automatically set to accommodate all the columns in the DataFrame.

Now that one of the most common ways to create a Pandas has been talked about, let us look at some of the other types you can pass to the DataFrame function to create the DataFrame.

- A dictionary of dictionaries: Converts each inner dictionary to columns and merges the keys to form a row index.

- Two-dimensional Numpy array: Creates a DataFrame using the passed data. You can pass row and column labels but this optional.

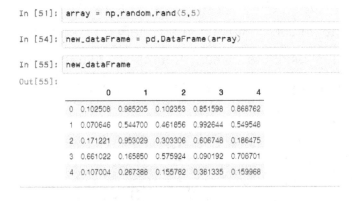

```
In [51]:  array = np.random.rand(5,5)

In [54]:  new_dataFrame = pd.DataFrame(array)

In [55]:  new_dataFrame
Out[55]:
                0          1          2          3          4
      0   0.102508   0.985205   0.102353   0.851598   0.868762
      1   0.070646   0.544700   0.461856   0.992644   0.549548
      2   0.171221   0.953029   0.303306   0.606748   0.186475
      3   0.661022   0.165850   0.575924   0.090192   0.708701
      4   0.107004   0.267388   0.155782   0.381335   0.159968
```

- Numpy Masked Array

- Another Pandas DataFrame

- List of dictionaries

- List of series

- Numpy Structured array

Pandas Series

A Pandas series refers to a one-dimensional array-like object that contains a series of values —similar to a Numpy array and an associated array of labels called an index. We can create the simplest Pandas series using a Numpy array as shown below:

```
In [2]: array = np.arange(0,20)

In [3]: series = pd.Series(array)

In [4]: series

Out[4]: 0    0
        1    1
        2    2
        3    3
        4    4
        5    5
```

```
In [2]: array = np.arange(0,20)

In [3]: series = pd.Series(array)

In [4]: series

Out[4]: 0    0
        1    1
        2    2
        3    3
        4    4
        5    5
```

The above prints a Pandas series with all values from the Numpy array – generated using the arange function – and the index. The output above shows the index of the Pandas series on the Left and the actual values on the right.

As we did not specify the index we want used, a default index made up of integers 0 through N − 1 - where N is the length of the data - is used. Using a Pandas series values and index attributes, we can also get the array representation and index object of the Pandas series.

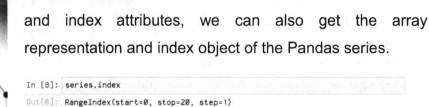

```
In [8]:  series.index
Out[8]:  RangeIndex(start=0, stop=20, step=1)

In [7]:  series.values  # use value attribute
Out[7]:  array([ 0,  1,  2,  3,  4,  5,  6,  7,  8,  9, 10, 11, 12, 13, 14, 15, 1
         6,
                17, 18, 19])
```

The best way is to create a Pandas series with index identifying each data point with a specified data label as shown:

```
In [9]:  indexed_Series = pd.Series([100,250,400,550,700], index=['OR','MI','MA','CA','VE'])

In [10]: indexed_Series
Out[10]: OR     100
         MI     250
         MA     400
         CA     550
         VE     700
         dtype: int64
```

For Pandas series, we can use the data labels in the index to select a single of a group of specific values.

```
In [12]:  indexed_Series['CA']
Out[12]:  550
```

This case is also true while selecting multiple elements using their respective indices.

```
In [13]:  indexed_Series[['CA','OR','MA']]

Out[13]:  CA      550
          OR      100
          MA      400
          dtype: int64
```

In the code above, the arguments ['CA', 'OR,' 'MA] interpret as a list of indices although it contains string type instead of integers.

It is also good to note that using Numpy operations or Numpy-like operations such as logical filtering, scalar multiplication, or mathematical functions call will not alter the index values:

```
In [15]:  np.exp(indexed_Series)

Out[15]:  OR        2.688117e+43
          MI        3.746455e+108
          MA        5.221470e+173
          CA        7.277212e+238
          VE        1.014232e+304
          dtype: float64
```

As you can see, doing this preserves the indices of the elements while it subjects the actual values to a mathematical exponential function.

You can also think of a Pandas series as a dictionary of fixed length where the indices represent the keys of dictionaries and the actual values are the array elements.

You can also pass a normal python dictionary to the Pandas Series function to create a series of elements.

```
In [19]: my_dict = {"OR": 100, "MI": 250, "MA": 400, "CA": 550, "VE": 700}

In [20]: pd.Series(my_dict)
Out[20]: OR    100
         MI    250
         MA    400
         CA    550
         VE    700
         dtype: int64
```

```
In [22]: indexed_Series.index = ['A','B','C','D','E']

In [23]: indexed_Series
Out[23]: A    100
         B    250
         C    400
         D    550
         E    700
         dtype: int64
```

A Pandas series assigns a value of NaN (Not a Number) to missing values. If a value is missing an index, the Pandas Series does not include it. We use the functions isnull and notnull to detect missing data.

Indexing, Selection, and Slicing

We can use the Pandas series indexing technique to select subsections of the Pandas DataFrame. Example:

```
In [57]:  dataFrame["Years"]
Out[57]:
          Barack Obama              8
          Abraham Lincoln          4
          John F Kennedy           2
          George Washington        8
          Franklin Roosevelt      12
          Name: Years, dtype: int64
```

NOTE: This only selects the integral section of the DataFrame.

Slicing a Pandas data structure, however, behaves differently from the usual python slicing technique as the end value is inclusive.

CHAPTER - 7

DATA VISUALIZATION WITH PYTHON

Histogram Plotting

The histogram plots are normally utilized for summarizing the distribution of data samples. The x-axis of the plots represents discrete bins and intervals for their observations. For instance, the observations having values between 1 and 10 are split into 5 bins and the values [1,2} will be allocated to the first bins, next [3.4] are allocated to your 2nd bean and so on. Y-axis of the plot represents a frequency or a count of the number of observations in your data sets that belong to every bin. Typically, the data sample is transformed into the bar chart when each category of the x-axis is representing an interval of various observation values.

Histograms are also termed as density estimates. The density estimates provide a good impression of the data distribution. The whole idea is to represent the data density locally by counting the number of observations inside a sequence with consecutive intervals or bins. The histogram plots are created by calling the function hist() and passing it in an array or list that represents your data sample.

Box Plots

The whisker and box plots and they are also called box plots, in short, are generally utilized for summarizing the data sample distribution. The x-axes are utilized for representing the data samples while several box plots are drawn side by side on the x-axis in case they are required. Y-axis will represent the observation values. The box gets drawn for summarizing the middle half portion of data sets. This starts at the 25% stage and ends at eh 75% stage. Middle of this is the 50% stage and it is drawn by a line. There is a value called interquartile range or IQR. This is calculated as 1.5 times the difference between 25% and 75% values. The lines are called whiskers and they are drawn for the extension from both ends of your box with the IQR length for demonstration of an expected range of sensible values inside the distribution. Any observations out of the whiskers will be outliers and they are drawn by using small circles.

Box plots are graphical techniques used for the display of variable distribution. It helps in getting the location, spread, skewness, tile length, and outlying points. This box plot would be a graphical representation of your five number summaries. The box plots are drawn by placing a call to the boxplot() function and passing data samples as in the case of lists or arrays.

A scatter plot

The next type of plot that we are going to take some time to look at is a scatter plot. Even though to someone who is not looking that closely, it may seem like this is a random table with lots of dots, it is actually going to be a visualization tool of your data that is pretty powerful and can be used to show us a lot of information. Basically, this is going to be a data visualization tool that is two dimensional and will rely on dots to show us more of the values that have been obtained for two separate types of variables. One is going to be plotted using the X-axis, and the other one is going to be plotted along the y-axis.

Each of the dots that show up in the scatter plot is going to be important, and we need to use all of them to understand what is going on with the graphs and information that we are using. The information that comes with it is going to depend on what you are trying to learn. For example, if we are doing a scatterplot to show us the weight and height of children, we would see that the height of the child would be found on the x-axis, and then the weight is going to be measured using the y-axis.

With this understanding, we need to be able to look at the times when we would use these scatter plots, rather than relying on some of the other options that are out there. These kinds of scatter plots are going to be used any time that we would like to show there is a relationship that happens between our two variables.

A good way to look at these scatter plots is how they are sometimes called correlation plots, mainly because they are going to show us the correlation between two variables. Going back to the weight and height example that we talked about before, the chart wasn't just going to be a log of the weight and height of those children, but it is going to show us, in a visual form, the relationship between the weight and height. As we can guess, even before looking at the information in this case, when the weight increases, the height increases in children.

Now, while we often look at the linear forms of the scatter plots, it is important to note that not all of the relationships that you are going to encounter with this one are going to be linear. A good example of this one would be the average daily high temperature that is measured over seven years, showing a familiar parabolic relationship that happens between these variables where the temperature is going to be lower in the winter and the go back up again in the summer. And it is also possible for the data that you are using to have no kind of discernible relationship at all, which on its own can be interesting because it shows that all of your data doesn't have a correlation.

In addition to this, it is possible to have a few common extensions that go with the scatter plots. Often these are going to include some kind of trendline that helps us to see the relationship a bit better and can give us kind of the median when it comes to the chosen information. We may also find that the color, the shape, and the size of the dot could represent a third, and sometimes even a fourth, variable on the information. You could change up the different dots in the height and weight category into those who are male and those who are female, to see the differences that could occur between the two genders when it comes to their height and weight.

The scatter plots can be a useful tool when it is time for us to look at the relationship that forms between two variables, but you have to have a good idea of how you can use these, and how you can interpret them in the proper manner. With this in mind, the code below is going to be used to help you create one of these scatter plots on your own system using the data that you already have available:

```
import numpy as np

import matplotlib.pyplot as plt

import matplotlib.cbook as cbook

# Load a numpy record array from yahoo csv data with fields date, open, close,

# volume, adj_close from the mpl-data/example directory. The record array

# stores the date as an np.datetime64 with a day unit ('D') in the date column.

with cbook.get_sample_data('goog.npz') as datafile:

price_data =
np.load(datafile)['price_data'].view(np.recarray)
```

```
price_data = price_data[-250:] # get the most recent 250
trading days

delta1 = np.diff(price_data.adj_close) /
price_data.adj_close[:-1]

# Marker size in units of points^2

volume = (15 * price_data.volume[:-2] /
price_data.volume[0])**2

close = 0.003 * price_data.close[:-2] / 0.003 *
price_data.open[:-2]

fig, ax = plt.subplots()

ax.scatter(delta1[:-1], delta1[1:], c=close, s=volume,
alpha=0.5)

ax.set_xlabel(r'$\Delta_i$', fontsize=15)

ax.set_ylabel(r'$\Delta_{i+1}$', fontsize=15)

ax.set_title('Volume and percent change')

ax.grid(True)

fig.tight_layout()

plt.show()
```

Visualisation with Seaborn

It is another Python data visualization library that is based on the popular one Matplotlib. Seaborn gives you a high level interface for the creation of attractive graphs. This library has plenty to offer. It is possible to create graphs in one line that will take several tens of lines for the Matplotlib. The standard designs used here are very useful and it also comes with a terrific interface for working with pandas. This library may be imported by typing:

import seaborn as sns

Heatmap

It is another graphical data representation where the independent values contained within a matrix are represented in the form of colors. The Heatmaps are ideal for the exploration of co-relations of features for the dataset. For acquiring the co-relations of the features within a data set you can call

```
<dataset>.corr()
```

It is a method used by Pandas data frame. It will provide you a co-relation matrix. You might utilize either Seaborn or Matplotlib for the creation of Heatmaps.

CHAPTER - 8

MACHINE LEARNING WITH PYTHON

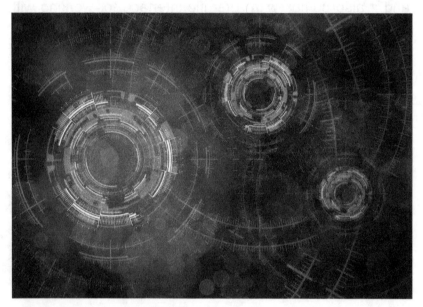

What is Machine Learning?

The first thing that we need to take a look at here is the basics of machine learning. This is going to be one of the techniques that we can use with data analytics that will help teach a computer how to learn and react on their own, without the interaction of the programmer. Many of the actions that we will train the system to do will be similar to actions that already come naturally to humans, such as learning from experience.

The algorithms that come with machine learning are going to be able to use computational methods in order to learn information right from the data, without having to rely on an equation that is predetermined as its model. The algorithms are going to adaptively improve some of their own performance as the number of samples that we will use for learning will increase.

There are a lot of instances where we are able to use machine learning. With the rise in big data that is available for all industries to use, We will find that machine learning is going to become one of the big techniques that are used to solve a ton of problems in many areas, including the following:

1. Computational finance: This is going to include algorithmic trading, credit scoring, and fraud detection.

2. Computer vision and other parts of image processing. This can be used in some different parts like object detection, motion detection, and face recognition.

3. Computational biology. This is going to be used for a lot of different parts, including DNA sequencing, drug discovery, and tumor detection.

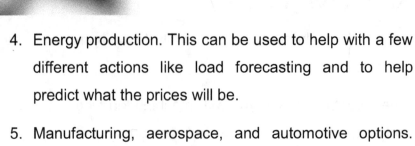

4. Energy production. This can be used to help with a few different actions like load forecasting and to help predict what the prices will be.

5. Manufacturing, aerospace, and automotive options. This is going to be a great technique to work with when it comes to helping with many parts, including predictive maintenance.

6. Natural language processing: This is going to be the way that we can use machine learning to help with applications of voice recognition.

Machine learning and the algorithms that they control are going to work by finding some natural patterns in the data that you can use, including using it in a manner that will help us to make some better predictions and decisions along the way. They are going to be used on a daily basis by businesses and a lot of different companies in order to make lots of critical decisions.

For example, medical facilities can use this to help them to help diagnose patients. And we will find that there are a lot of media sites that will rely on machine learning in order to sift through the potential of millions of options in order to give recommendations to the users. Retailers can use this as a way to gain some insight into the purchasing behavior of their customers along the way.

There are many reasons that your business is able to consider using machine learning. For example, it is going to be useful if you are working with a task that is complex or one that is going to involve a larger amount of data and a ton of variables, but there isn't an equation or a formula that is out there right now to handle it. For example, some of the times when we want to work with machine learning include:

1. Equations and rules that are hand-written and too complex to work with. This could include some options like speech recognition and face recognition.

2. When you find that the rules that are going to change all of the time. This could be seen in actions lie fraud detection from a large number of transactional records.

3. When you find that the nature of your data is going to change on a constant basis, and the program has to be able to adapt along the way. This could be seen when we work with predicting the trends during shopping when doing energy demand forecasting and even automated trading, to name a few.

As you can see, there are a lot of different things that we are able to do when it comes to machine learning, and pretty much any industry is going to be able to benefit from working with this for their own needs. Machine learning is more complex, but we are able to combine it together with Python in order to get some amazing results in the process and to ensure that our data analysis is going to work the way that we want.

Decision trees and Random forests

Decision trees: A decision tree algorithm tries to classify the elements by identifying questions concerning their attributes that will assist decide of which class to place them. Each node inside the tree is a question, with branches that lead to more questions about the articles, and the leaves as the final classifications.

Use cases for decision trees can include the construction of knowledge management platforms for customer service, price predictions, and product planning.

An insurance agency could utilize a decision tree when it requires data about the sort of protection items and the excellent changes dependent on possible hazard, says Ray Johnson, boss information researcher at business and innovation counseling firm SPR. Utilizing area information overlaid with climate related misfortune information, you can make hazard classes dependent on claims made and cost sums. It would then be able to assess new models of fence against models to give a hazard class and a potential monetary effect, the official said.

Random Forests: A decision tree must be prepared to give precise outcomes, the irregular timberland calculation takes a lot of irregular choice trees that base their choices on various arrangements of attributes and permit them to cast a ballot in the most well-known request.

Random forests are simply flexible devices for discovering connections in data sets and quick to train, says Epstein. For example, unsolicited bulk mail has been a problem for a long time, not only for users but also for Internet service providers that have to manage the increased load on servers. In response to this problem, automated methods have been developed to filter spam from standard email, using random forests to quickly and accurately identify unwanted emails, the executive said.

Other uses of random forests include the identification of disease by analyzing the patient's medical records, detecting bank fraud, predicting the volume of calls in the call centers and predicting gains or losses through the Purchase of a particular stock.

SciKit-Learn

This is a fundamental tool used in data-mining and data analysis related tasks. This is an open-source tool and licensed under BSD. This tool can be accessed or reused in different contexts. SciKit has been developed on top of NumPy, Matplotlib, and SciPy. The tool is utilized for classification, regression, and clustering and managing spam, image recognition, stock pricing, drug response, and customer segmentation, etc. The tool also permits model selection, dimensionality reduction, and pre-processing.

Linear Regression

The word "linearity" in algebra implies a linear connection between two or more variables. If we draw this connection in a two-dimensional space (amongst two variables), we get a conservative line.

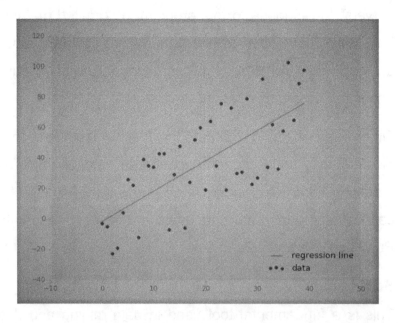

Linear regression completes the duty to foresee a dependent variable rate (y) built on a certain independent variable (x). So, this regression method finds out a linear connection between x (input) in addition to y (output).

Thus, they term it the Linear Regression. If we plot the dependent and independent variable (y and x) on their axis, linear regression gives us a conventional line that fits the information plugs as revealed in the picture below. We then recognize that the equation of a conventional line is essential.

The equation of the overhead line is:

Y= mx + b

Where b is the advert and m are the hills of the line. So, essentially, the linear regression algorithm gives us the greatest ideal rate for the advert and the hill (in two magnitudes). Although the y and x variables produce the result, they are the data structures and cannot be altered. The figures that we can switch are the advert(b) and hill(m). There can be numerous conventional lines relying upon the figures of the advert and the figures of the hill. Essentially, what the linear regression algorithm ensures is it fits numerous lines on the data points and yields the line that results in the slightest mistake.

This similar idea can be stretched to cases where there are additional variables. This is termed numerous linear regressions. For example, think about a situation where you must guess the price of the house built upon its extent, the number of bedrooms, the regular income of the people in the area, the oldness of the house, and so on. In this situation, the dependent variable (target variable) is reliant on numerous independent variables. A regression model including numerous variables can be signified as:

y = b0 + m1b1 + m2b2 + m3b3 + ... mnbn

This is the comparison of a hyperplane. Recall that a linear regression model in two magnitudes is a straight line; in three magnitudes it is a plane, and in additional magnitudes, a hyperplane.

Support Vector Machines (SVM)

A managed algorithm used for machine learning which can mutually be employed for regression or classification challenges is Support Vector Machines. Nevertheless, it is typically employed in classification complications. In this algorithm, we design each data entry as a point in n-dimensional space (where n is many structures you have) with the rate of each feature being the rate of a coordinate. Then, we complete the classification by finding the hyper-plane that distinguishes the two classes very well.

Look at the image below:

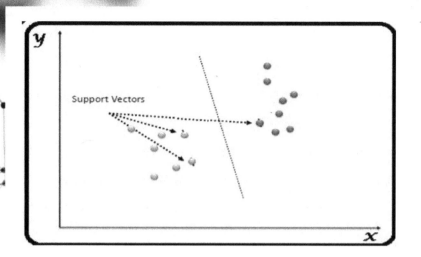

Support Vectors are the coordinates of separate thoughts. Support Vector Machine is a borderline that best isolates the two classes (hyper-plane/ line).

K-means Clustering

The 2000 and 2004 Constitutional determinations in the United States were closed. The highest percentage received by any runner from a general ballot was 50.7% and the lowest was 47.9%. If a proportion of the electorates were to have their sides swapped, the result of the determination would have been dissimilar. There are small clusters of electorates who, when appropriately enticed, will change sides. These clusters may not be gigantic, but with such close competitions, they might be big enough to change the result of the determination. By what means do you find these clusters of individuals? By what means do you petition them with an inadequate budget? To do this, you can employ clustering.

Let us recognize how it is done.

- First, you gather data on individuals either with or without their permission: any kind of data that might give an approximate clue about what is vital to them and what will affect how they vote.
- Then you set this data into a clustering algorithm.
- Next, for each group (it would be very nifty to select the principal one first), you create a letter that will appeal to these electorates.
- Lastly, you send the campaign and measure to see if it's employed.

Clustering is a category of unsupervised learning that routinely makes clusters of comparable groups. It is like an involuntary classification. You can cluster nearly everything, and the more comparable the objects are in the cluster, the enhanced the clusters are.

Naïve Bayes

The Naïve Bayes algorithm is a good choice to go with when you want to do a bit of exploration with the data in the beginning. Maybe you want to see what the best way is to split up the data that you have, or you are not yet certain about what kind of algorithm is going to be the best one for you to focus your attention on yet. In some cases, you may need to show some of the data and some of the information that you have ahead of time, right after collecting it, to those who want to see what is going on, but may not understand all of the more technical aspects that come with it.

This is where the Naïve Bayes algorithm is going to come into play and can really help us. With this option, we are able to take a good exploration of the data that we have, and then determine the best steps to take after. Sometimes this helps us to choose which of the other algorithms are the best ones for us to go with. And other times, it may be a good way to create a beginner's model so that we can show this off before being able to finish all of the work for the final project.

The Naïve Bayes algorithm is usually not going to be the first choice that we make when it is time to handle some of our data, and we will usually go through and make a few other adjustments to the process as well and finish off with another kind of algorithm. But it is definitely a good algorithm to go with because it adds in a lot of the different parts that you need to get a good idea about what the data contains, and what else we are able to do with it along the way.

CHAPTER - 9

APPLICATIONS OF MACHINE LEARNING

Deep Learning

The first topic that we need to dive into here is what deep learning is all about. Deep learning is considered a function that comes with artificial intelligence, one that is able to imitate, as closely as possible, some of the workings we see in the human brain when it comes to creating patterns and processing complex data to use with decision making. Basically, we can use the parts of deep learning to help us take our machine or our system and teach it how to think through things the same way that a human can, although at a faster and more efficient rate.

So, to get a better idea of how this is going to benefit us, we first need to take a look at how we can work with deep learning. The process of deep learning has really evolved a lot in the past few years, going hand in hand with a lot of the things we have seen in the digital era. This time period has really brought about so much data, data that comes in so many forms. In particular, this data is known as big data, and we will be able to draw it out of a lot of different areas such as e-commerce platforms, search engines, social media, and more.

If a company uses some of the algorithms that come with machine learning, they will be able to actually use all of the information that they are collecting. They can use it to recommend products for their customers, to really work on making predictions and finding patterns with the information so they can really run their business the way that they would like.

You will notice though that this unstructured data is going to be pretty large, and for an employee to go through this information and get the relevant parts from it, it would take so long the information would no longer be relevant and useful. And by the time they did, the information would be old, and the world would have already moved on and

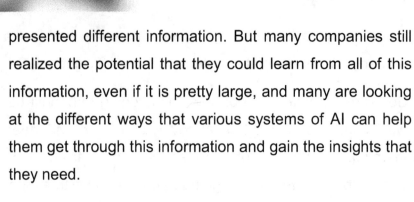

presented different information. But many companies still realized the potential that they could learn from all of this information, even if it is pretty large, and many are looking at the different ways that various systems of AI can help them get through this information and gain the insights that they need.

Look at how deep learning is going to work. Deep learning has evolved at the same time and often at the same pace as we see with the digital era. This is an era that has seen a big explosion of data in all forms, and from every region of the world. This is a lot of data, and it is there to help businesses make informed decisions that weren't possible in the past.

Think about all of the information that you already have at your fingertips, and you may not even realize that it is there. Before you even decide to start working with big data, you already know that if you need to look up something, you can head to your favorite search engine and it will all be there. Our digital era is bringing out a ton of new information and data, and the smart companies, the ones who would like to get ahead, are the ones who not only gather all of that data, but who learn how to use it.

This data, which is often called big data, is drawn from a variety of sources depending on what the business is trying to accomplish. These can come from places like ecommerce platforms, search engines, online cinemas, search engines, and more. The enormous amount of data that fits into the category of big data is going to be readily accessible to anyone who wants it, and it is possible to share it through a lot of different applications like cloud computing.

However, this data, which is normally going to come to us in a form that is unstructured, is so vast that if a person manually went through all of it, it may take decades to extract out the information that is relevant to what they need. Companies realize this, and they now that there is a lot of potential that can be found in all of that data that they have collected. And this is why creating and adapting artificial intelligence systems with automated support is something that many of them have started to focus their attention on.

Natural Language Processing

Have you noticed that more and more companies are putting a bot widget on their site? Chatbots are everywhere today. And of Natural Language Processing (NLP) and Natural Language Understanding (NLU) technologies. The potential of NLP and NLU seems limitless. Now everyone understands that we are only at the beginning of a long journey.

Titans in the IT industry are creating dedicated research departments to explore this area. Intel did not stand aside. Recently, Intel AI Lab released a product called NLP Architect. This is an open source library designed to serve as the basis for further research and collaboration of developers from around the world.

NLP Architect

A team of NLP researchers and developers from Intel AI Lab is studying the current architecture of deep neural networks and methods for processing and understanding text. The result of their work was a set of tools that are interesting from both a theoretical and an applied point of view.

Here's what the current version of NLP Architect has:

- Models that extract the linguistic characteristics of text: for example, a parser (BIST) and an algorithm for extracting nouns (noun phrases);

- State-of-the-art models for understanding the language: for example, determination of user intent (intent extraction), recognition of named entities (named entity recognition, NER);

- Modules for semantic analysis: for example, collocations, the most probable meaning of a word, vector representations of named groups (NP2V);

- Building blocks for creating conversational intelligence: for example, the basis for creating chatbots, including a dialogue support system, a sequence analyzer (sequence chunker), a system for determining the user's intent;

- Examples of using deep end-to-end neural networks with a new architecture: for example, question-answer systems, text reading systems (machine reading comprehension).

- For all of the above models, there are examples of learning and prediction processes. Moreover, the Intel team added scripts to solve typical tasks that arise when implementing such models - pipelines for data processing and utilities that are often used in NLP.

The library consists of separate modules, which simplifies integration. A general view of the NLP Architect framework is shown in the diagram below.

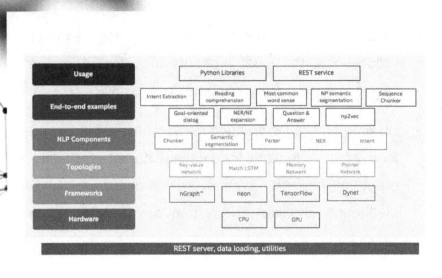

Usage		Python Libraries		REST service	
End-to-end examples	Intent Extraction	Reading comprehension	Most common word sense	NP semantic segmentation	Sequence Chunker
	Goal-oriented dialog	NER/NE expansion	Question & Answer	np2vec	
NLP Components	Chunker	Semantic segmentation	Parser	NER	Intent
Topologies	Key-value network	Match LSTM	Memory Network	Pointer Network	
Frameworks	nGraph™	neon	TensorFlow	Dynet	
Hardware		CPU	GPU		

REST server, data loading, utilities

NLP Architect Framework

Components for NLP / NLU

Offer analyzer. Analysis of sentences (sequence chunking) is one of the basic tasks of word processing, which consists in dividing sentences into syntactically related parts. For example, a sentence

"Little Sasha walked along the highway" can be divided into four parts: the nouns "Little Sasha" and "highway", the verb group "walked" and the prepositional group "by".

The analyzer of sentences from NLP Architect can build suitable neural network architecture for different types of input data: tokens, labels of parts of speech, vector representations, symbolic signs.

Semantic segmentation of noun groups. A noun phrase consists of the main member - a noun or pronoun - and several dependent qualifying members. To simplify, you can divide nouns into two types:

- With descriptive structure: dependent members do not significantly affect the semantics of the main member (for example, "sea water");

- With collocation structure: dependent members significantly change the meaning of the main term (for example, "guinea pig").

To determine the type of name group, a multilayer perceptron is trained. This model is used in the semantic sentence segmentation algorithm. As a result of her work, nouns of the first type break up into several semantic elements, and nouns of the second type remain unified.

The parser performs grammar analysis of sentences, examining the relationship between words in sentences and highlighting things like direct additions and predicates. NLP Architect includes a graph-based dependency parser that uses BiLSTM to extract features.

The Named Entity Recognizer (NER) identifies certain words or combinations of words in a text that belong to a certain class of interest to us. Examples of entities include names, numbers, places, currencies, dates, organizations.

Sometimes entities can be quite easily distinguished with the help of such features as the form of words, the presence of a word in a certain dictionary, part of speech. However, quite often these signs are not known to us or even exist. In such cases, in order to determine whether a word or phrase is an entity, it is necessary to analyze its context.

The model for NER in NLP Architect is based on a bidirectional LSTM network and CRF classifier. A high-level review of the model is presented below.

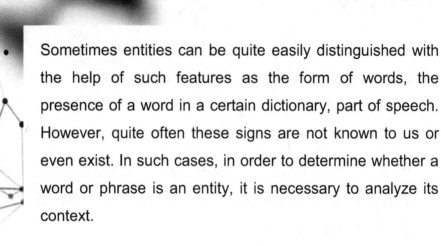

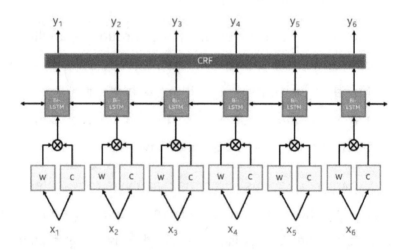

High Level Review of the NER Model

The user intent determination algorithm solves the problem of understanding the language. Its purpose is to understand what kind of action is discussed in the text, and to identify all parties involved. For example, for a sentence

"Siri, please remind me to pick up things from the laundry on the way home."

The algorithm determines the action ("remind"), who should perform this action ("Siri"), who asks to perform this action ("I") and the object of the action ("pick up things from the laundry").

The analyzer of the meaning of the word. The algorithm receives a word at the input and returns all the meanings of this word, as well as numbers characterizing the prevalence of each of the meanings in the language.

NLP Architect Visualizer

The library includes a small web server - NLP Architect Server. It makes it easy to test the performance of different NLP Architect models. Among other things, the server has visualizers, which are pretty nice diagrams that demonstrate the operation of the models. Currently, two services support visualization - a parser and a recognizer of named entities. In addition, there is a template with which the user can add visualization for other services.

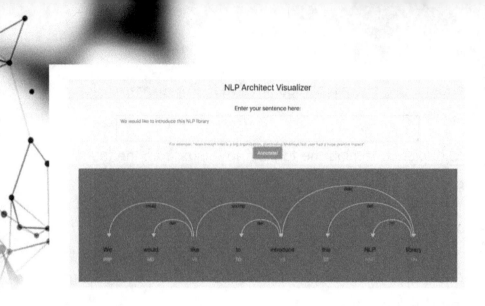

NLP Architect is an open and flexible library with algorithms for word processing, which makes it possible for developers from all over the world to interact. The Intel team continues to add the results of its research to the library so that anyone can take advantage of what they have done and improved.

To get started, just download the code from the Github repository and follow the installation instructions. Here you can find comprehensive documentation for all the main modules and ready-made models.

In future releases, Intel AI Lab plans to demonstrate the benefits of creating text analysis algorithms using the latest deep learning technologies, and include methods for extracting text tonality, analyzing topics and trends, expanding specialized vocabulary, and extracting relationships in the library. In addition, Intel experts are exploring teaching methods without teacher and partial training, with which you can create new interpretable models for understanding and analyzing text that can adapt to new areas of knowledge.

Neural Network

The first type of network we are going to look at is the "normal" type of neural network. These neural networks are going to fit into the category of unsupervised machine learning because they are able to work on their own and provide us with some great results in the process. Neural networks are a great option to work within machine learning because they are set up to catch onto any pattern or trend that is found in a set of data. This can be done through a variety of levels, and in a way that is going to be much faster and more effective than a human going through and doing the work manually.

When we work with a neural network, each of the layers that we will focus on are responsible for spending time in that layer, seeing if they are able to find a pattern or trend inside the image, or through the data, that it looks at. Once it has found a trend or a pattern, it is going to start its process for entering into the next layer. This process is going to continue, with the network finding a new pattern or trend, and then going on to the next level, until it reaches a place where there are no more trends or patterns to find.

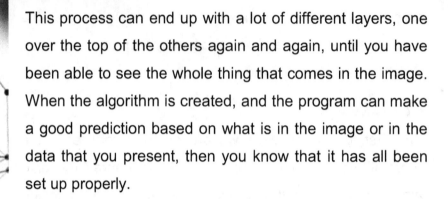

This process can end up with a lot of different layers, one over the top of the others again and again, until you have been able to see the whole thing that comes in the image. When the algorithm is created, and the program can make a good prediction based on what is in the image or in the data that you present, then you know that it has all been set up properly.

Before we move on though, we have to remember that there are a few parts that will start to occur at this point, based on how you set up the program to work. If the algorithm was able to read through all of the layers and the steps above, and it had success with reading through the different layers, then it is able to make a good prediction for you. If the algorithm is accurate with the prediction that it made, then the neurons that come with this algorithm will strengthen and become faster and more efficient at their job overall.

Keep in mind that the more times that the algorithm is able to provide the right answer during this process, the more efficient it will become when you try to use it another time as well. The neurons get stronger, and you will see that the answers come faster and are more accurate overall.

Now, if you haven't been able to work with machine learning and deep learning in the past, it may seem like these neural networks would be impossible to actually see happen. But a closer examination of these algorithms can help us to see better how they work and why they can be so important to this process. For the example that we are going to work with, let's say that we have a goal to make a program that can take the image we present, and then, by going through the different layers, the program is able to recognize that the image in that picture is actually a car.

If we have created the neural network in the proper manner, then it is able to take a look at the image that we use and make a good prediction that it sees a car in the picture. The program will then be able to come up with this prediction based on any features and parts that it already knows comes with a car. This could include things like the color, the license plate, the door placement, where the headlights are, and more.

When we take a look at coding with some of the traditional methods, whether they are Python methods or not, this is something that you may be able to do, but it takes way too long and is not the best option to work with. It can take a lot of coding and really just confuse up the whole process. But with these neural networks, you will be able to write out the codes to get this kind of network done in no time.

To get the neural network algorithm to work the way that you want, you have to provide the system with a good and clear image of a car. The network can then take a look at that picture and start going through some of the layers that it needs to work with to see the picture. So, the system will be able to go through the first layer, which may include something like the outside edges of the car. When it was done with this, the network would continue on from one layer to the next, going through however many layers it takes to complete the process and provide us with a good prediction. Sometimes this is just a few layers, but the more layers this program can go through, the more likely it will provide an accurate prediction in the end.

Depending on the situation or the project that you want to work with, there is the potential for adding in many different layers. The good news with this one is that the more details and the more layers that a neural network can find, the more accurately it can predict what object is in front of it, and even what kind of car it is looking at.

As the neural network goes through this process, and it shows a result that is accurate when identifying the car model, it is actually able to learn from that lesson, similar to what we see with the human brain. The neural network is set up in a way to remember the patterns and the different characteristics that it saw in the car model, and con store onto that information to use at another time if it encounters another car that is the same again. So, if you present, at a later time, another image with that same car model in it, then the neural network can make a prediction on that image fairly quickly.

There are several options that you can choose to use this kind of system for, but remember that each time you make a neural network, it is only able to handle one task at a time. you can make a neural network that handles facial recognition for example, and one that can find pictures that we need in a search engine, but you can't make one neural network do all of the tasks that you want. You may have to split it up and make a few networks to see this happen.

For example, there is often a lot of use for neural networks when it comes to creating software that can recognize faces. All of the information that you need to create this kind of network would not be available ahead of time, so the neural network will be able to learn along the way and get better with recognizing the faces that it sees in video or images. This is also a method that can be effective when you would like to get it to recognize different animals or recognize a specific item in other images or videos as well.

To help us out here, we need to take a look at some of the advantages that can come with this kind of model with machine learning. One of the advantages that a lot of programmers like with this one is that you can work with

this algorithm without having to be in total control over the statistics of the algorithm. Even if you are not working with statistics all of the time, or you are not really familiar with how to use them, you will see that these networks can be used without those statistics, still that if there is any relationship, no matter how complex it is, is inside the information, then it is going to show up when you run the network.

The nice thing with this one is that the relationships inside your data can be found, whether the variables are dependent or independent, and even if you are working with variables that do not follow a linear path. This is good information for those who are just getting started with machine learning because it ensures that we can get a better understanding of how the data relates to each other, and some of the insights that you want to work with, no matter what variables you are working with.

With this in mind, we have to remember that there are still times when we will not use a neural network, and it will not be the solution to every problem that we want to handle in deep learning. One of the bigger issues that come with these neural network algorithms, and why some programmers decide to not use this is that the computing costs are going to be kind of high.

This is an algorithm that is pretty in-depth, and because of this, the computing costs are going to be a bit higher than what we find with some of the other options out there. and for some businesses, and even on some of the projects that you want to do with deep learning, this computation cost will just be too high. It will take on too much power, too much money, and often too much time. For some of the projects that you want to take on, the neural networks will be a great addition to your arsenal with deep learning, and other times, you may want to go another route.

Neural networks are a great option to work with when it is time to expand out your work and when you would like to create a program that can handle some more complex activities. With the right steps here, and with some time to train the neural network, you will find that the neural network is a great way to handle your data and find the trends and predictions that you want.

Clustering

Clustering algorithms use techniques such as K-means, mean-shift, or expectation-maximation to group data points based on shared or related characteristics, this is an unsupervised learning method that can be applied to the classification problems.

Clustering technique is particularly useful when you need to segment or categorize, Schatsky notes. Examples

include segmenting customers by different characteristics to assign marketing campaigns better, recommending news articles to confident readers, and effective law enforcement.

The clustering is likewise dynamic for discovering clusters in complex informational indexes that may not be evident to the natural eye. Examples range from the categorization of similar documents in a database to the identification of critical crime points in crime reports, says Epstein.

CONCLUSION

This is the end of the book. The next milestone is to make the best use of your new-found wisdom of Python programming, data science, data analysis, and machine learning that have resulted in the birth of the powerhouse, which is the "Silicon Valley." So many companies, that span a lot of different industries, are able to benefit when they work with data analysis. This allows them to get a lot of the power and control that they want for their respective industries and will ensure that they will be able to really impress their customers and get some good results in the process. Learning how to use a data analysis is going to change the game in how you do business, as long as it is used in the proper manner.

This guidebook has been organized well to explore what data analysis is all about, and how we are able to use this for our benefits as well. There are a lot of business tools out there, but data analysis is designed to help us focus on finding the hidden patterns and insights that are in our data, making it easier to base our decisions on data, rather than intuition and guessing as we did in the past. And when it comes to making sure that we complete the data analysis in the right manner, nothing is better than working with the Python coding language to get things done.

There are so many aspects that need to come into play when we are working with our own data analysis, and it is important that we take the time to learn how these works, and how to put it all together. And that is exactly what we will do in this guidebook. When you are ready to learn more about Python data analysis, and all of the different parts that come together to help us with understanding our data and how to run our business, make sure to recheck this guide to help you.

You would also develop skills in loading and exporting dataset from and to Python environments. You would also acquire skills in analysis and processing datasets using both libraries NumPy and Pandas by handling missing data and exploring datasets. You would develop skill in visualizing data using different type of graphs as well by mastering the functionalities of the matplotlib library.

Overall this book provides a guide on using these handy libraries in data analysis. Once you have acquired these skills and know the functionalities of the NumPy, Pandas and Matplotlib libraries, you will be able to analyze any data you have in hand using Python. You also develop more advanced skills to handle complex datasets.

Now that you have finished reading this book and mastered the use of Python programming, you are all set to start developing your own Python based machine learning model as well as performing big data analysis using all the open sources readily available and explicitly described in this book. You can position yourself to use your deep knowledge and understanding of all the cutting edge technologies obtained from this book to contribute to the growth of any company and land yourself a new high paying and rewarding job!